GOOD PRACTICE NOTE ON ADDRESSING SEXUAL EXPLOITATION, ABUSE, AND HARASSMENT IN ADB-FINANCED PROJECTS WITH CIVIL WORKS

APRIL 2023

ADB

ASIAN DEVELOPMENT BANK

© 2023 Asian Development Bank
6 ADB Avenue, Mandaluyong City, 1550 Metro Manila, Philippines
Tel +63 2 8632 4444; Fax +63 2 8636 2444
www.adb.org

Some rights reserved. Published in 2023.

ISBN 978-92-9270-079-9 (print); 978-92-9270-080-5 (electronic); 978-92-9270-081-2 (ebook)
Publication Stock No. TIM230093-2
DOI: http://dx.doi.org/10.22617/TIM230093-2

The views expressed in this publication are those of the authors and do not necessarily reflect the views and policies of the Asian Development Bank (ADB) or its Board of Governors or the governments they represent.

ADB does not guarantee the accuracy of the data included in this publication and accepts no responsibility for any consequence of their use. The mention of specific companies or products of manufacturers does not imply that they are endorsed or recommended by ADB in preference to others of a similar nature that are not mentioned.

By making any designation of or reference to a particular territory or geographic area, or by using the term "country" in this publication, ADB does not intend to make any judgments as to the legal or other status of any territory or area.

Please contact pubsmarketing@adb.org if you have questions or comments with respect to content, or if you wish to obtain copyright permission for your intended use that does not fall within these terms, or for permission to use the ADB logo.

Corrigenda to ADB publications may be found at http://www.adb.org/publications/corrigenda.

Cover design by Cleone Baradas.

Contents

Tables, Figures, and Boxes

Acknowledgments

This good practice note (GPN) is part of the efforts of the Asian Development Bank (ADB) to strengthen operational approaches to addressing risks of sexual exploitation, abuse, and harassment (SEAH) in ADB-financed operations with a specific focus on sovereign projects with civil works.

Malika Shagazatova, social development specialist (gender and development) with ADB's Sustainable Development and Climate Change Department (SDCC), led the development of this GPN with support from Wilma Silva-Netto Rojas, national consultant; and Noel Chavez, senior operations assistant (gender and development), SDCC. Social Development Direct, particularly Danielle Cornish-Spencer, prepared the draft GPN and the toolkit. This GPN was edited by Caroline Ahmad, and graphics and layout were done by Cleone Baradas and Joe Mark Ganaban, respectively.

Consultations with ADB departments and relevant resident missions have been of significant value and many ADB staff members provided valuable comments and inputs to this publication. ADB's SEAH Task Force Team has played a key role in developing ADB's operational approaches. The team gratefully acknowledges Patricia Rhee and Melinda Tun of the Office of the General Counsel; Rubina Shaheen of the Procurement, Portfolio and Financial Management Department; Ashish Bhateja of the Strategy, Policy and Partnerships Department; and January Agbon Sanchez and Jacqueline Bell of the Office of Anticorruption and Integrity for their significant contribution and support for the development and finalization of this GPN.

Special thanks to Samantha Hung, chief of gender equality thematic group with SDCC, for overall support and guidance throughout the process.

Abbreviations

ADB	Asian Development Bank
DMC	developing member country
GBV	gender-based violence
GPN	good practice note
GRM	grievance redress mechanism
MDB	multilateral development bank
MGPS	minimum good practice standards
NGO	nongovernment organization
SDG	Sustainable Development Goals
SEAH	sexual exploitation, abuse, and harassment
SOP	standard operating procedures
TOR	terms of reference

Preamble

The Asian Development Bank (ADB) developed this good practice note (GPN) to assist ADB staff, executing and implementing agency staff, and consultants in identifying risks of sexual exploitation, abuse, and harassment (SEAH) in selected ADB-financed sovereign projects with civil works;[1] and to advise executing and implementing agencies on how to best prevent, mitigate, and respond to such risks.[2]

This GPN is not an ADB policy or a policy-triggered mandatory procedure. Its recommendations are advisory. They apply only to new sovereign projects with civil works, in selected ADB developing member countries (DMCs), for a pilot period designated by ADB. As this GPN applies only during the pilot period, the GPN, and its application to new sovereign projects during this period, is not subject to ADB's Accountability Mechanism. In addition, the recommendations in this GPN do not apply to policy-based loans, results-based loans, or financial intermediation loans. ADB is developing an accompanying GPN on integrating SEAH reporting and case handling into grievance redress mechanisms (GRMs) in ADB projects with civil works that will lay out recommendations on good practices for SEAH response and reporting in more detail.[3] A separate GPN to provide guidance on prevention, mitigation, and response to SEAH in ADB's private sector operations is also forthcoming (footnote 3).

Following the pilot period, this GPN may be updated to reflect lessons learned and emerging good practices. ADB is fully cognizant of the operational risks associated with SEAH, and the ongoing review of ADB's Safeguard Policy Statement (2009) will consider SEAH and be guided by stakeholder consultations. In the event SEAH is incorporated into a revised Safeguards Policy Standards, this GPN will be updated further as necessary as a guidance note or good practice note to support new ADB's Safeguards Policy implementation.

---

[1] New sovereign projects are defined as sovereign projects with concept papers approved after the launch date of the pilot. For this GPN, civil works are defined as those large enough to be carried out by a contractor and include construction, upgrading, and/or maintenance works within ADB-financed projects and sectors of operations.

[2] The GPN draws on international experience and global good practice, especially that of other multilateral development banks (MDBs) and bilateral partners, and is informed by global research.

[3] ADB. Forthcoming. *Good Practice Note on Integrating Sexual Exploitation, Abuse, and Harassment Reporting and Case Handling into Project Grievance Redress Mechanisms in ADB-Financed Projects with Civil Works (Sovereign Operations)*. Manila.

This GPN will use the definition of SEAH in Box 1. Annex A contains a full list of key concepts.

BOX 1
Sexual Exploitation, Abuse, and Harassment Defined

Although sexual exploitation, abuse, and harassment (SEAH) can happen anywhere in society, when used as an umbrella term within official development assistance (ODA), the term refers to acts of SEAH perpetrated by those working in, with, or through, ODA actors and their projects.[a]

Service users, community members, and staff working in ODA are vulnerable to being targeted for SEAH (footnote a) Definitions are as follows:

Sexual exploitation	Any actual or attempted abuse of a position of vulnerability, differential power, or trust for sexual purposes, including profiting monetarily, socially, or politically from the sexual exploitation of another.[b]
Sexual abuse	The actual or threatened physical intrusion of a sexual nature, whether by force or unequal or coercive conditions.[b]
Sexual harassment	Any unwelcome conduct of a sexual nature that might reasonably be expected or be perceived to cause offense or humiliation, when such conduct interferes with work, is made a condition of employment, or creates an intimidating, hostile, or offensive work environment.[c] Sexual harassment can occur outside the workplace and outside working hours, including during official travel, social functions related to work, and online. Sexual harassment does not need to be between colleagues and can occur within society in general.

[a] Adapted from Resource and Support Hub. 2021. *Understanding SEAH and GBV* [gender-based violence]. Resource & Support Hub, UK Aid.
[b] Task Team on the SEA [Sexual Exploitation and Abuse] Glossary for the Special Coordinator on improving the United Nations response to sexual exploitation and abuse. 2017. *Glossary on Sexual Exploitation and Abuse* (second edition).
[c] United Nations Secretariat. 2019. *Addressing Discrimination, Harassment, Including Sexual Harassment, and Abuse of Authority*. Secretary-General's bulletin ST/SGB/2019/8. New York.
Source: Asian Development Bank.

INTRODUCTION

All project-affected populations, employees of executing and implementing agencies, and contractors working on ADB-financed projects should feel safe from SEAH. SEAH is an endemic issue within society and is perpetrated in all spheres of life. This GPN is intended to assist in the identification of risks of SEAH that may occur in ADB sovereign projects with civil works in designated pilot DMCs, and to advise executing and implementing agencies on how to best manage such risks, including by putting in place resources and guidance to prevent and mitigate SEAH and respond appropriately.

During the 2018 Safeguarding Summit on tackling SEAH in the international aid sector, 10 international financial institutions, including ADB, reaffirmed their commitment to preventing SEAH through seven principles (Box 2) and vowed to undertake periodic joint reporting.[4]

BOX 2

Seven Principles within the International Financial Institutions Framework

1 Foster a culture of respect and high standards of ethical behavior across institutions.

2 Establish and maintain standards aimed at preventing sexual harassment, abuse, and exploitation and other forms of misconduct.

3 Provide a safe and trusted environment for those affected by sexual harassment, abuse, and exploitation to step forward to report incidents and concerns, with the assurance that they will be treated respectfully and consistently.

4 Provide protection for those affected, as well as whistleblowers and/or witnesses within their institutions, and take appropriate measures against any form of retaliation.

5 Maintain robust policy frameworks and clear institutional mechanisms that address how incidents and allegations will be handled should they arise.

6 Provide effective training programs so all staff understand the requirements and standards of behavior expected of them as international civil servants.

7 Support clients to develop and implement policies and mechanisms that address sexual harassment, abuse, and exploitation.

Source: IFI Update on the Joint Statement on Continuous Advancement of Standards to Prevent Sexual Harassment, Abuse, and Exploitation.

---

[4] Government of the United Kingdom, Department for International Development and Foreign, Commonwealth and Development Office. 2018. *International Financial Institutions: Commitments to Tackle Sexual Exploitation and Abuse and Sexual Harassment In the International Aid Sector*. London.

Addressing SEAH is a priority for ADB. As a signatory to the 2018 summit, ADB agreed to the following long-term commitments:

- ◗ Ensure support for survivors and whistleblowers, enhance accountability and transparency, strengthen reporting, and tackle impunity.

- ◗ Incentivize cultural change through strong leadership, organizational accountability, and better human resource processes.

- ◗ Adopt global standards and ensure they are met or exceeded.

- ◗ Strengthen organizational capacity and capability across the international aid sector to meet these standards.

This GPN is intended to provide practical guidance to contribute to ADB meeting the seven commitments listed in Box 2 with respect to ADB-financed sovereign projects with civil works.

Box 3 provides a short history of SEAH in official development assistance operations.[5]

---

[5] For a more detailed overview of the history and background of sexual exploitation and abuse, see Appendixes 1 and 2 in S. Martin. 2005. *Must Boys Be Boys?* (First edition). Refugees International.

BOX 3

A Short History of Sexual Exploitation, Abuse, and Harassment in Official Development Assistance Operations

Sexual exploitation and abuse (SEA) has been documented to have been perpetrated in relation to development assistance since the 1960s.[a] However, it was not until public attention was drawn to the issue in the early 1990s that development and humanitarian actors devised policies that prohibit this behavior.[b] The acronym SEA was originally most commonly used within official development assistance operations in relation to United Nations peacekeepers in humanitarian contexts.

From 2015 onward, several scandals involving perpetration and cover-up of sexual exploitation, abuse, and harassment (SEAH) across a wide range of contexts and development actors made headlines across the world.[c] During this time, sexual harassment was added to the definition of SEAH.[d] Harassment in the workplace, harassment of beneficiaries of official development assistance, and harassment on the journey to and from work have been added to definitions of SEAH within international development assistance. This expansion of scope was driven by an acknowledgment that harassment sits within the same continuum of violence as sexual exploitation and sexual abuse.

As well as the ethical imperative to address SEAH within international development assistance, it is important to note that there are other risks associated with not addressing SEAH including a reduction in public support for international development assistance because of erosion of public confidence, reputational risks, and risks to projects being successfully implemented on time and on budget.

The renewed focus on SEAH resulted in the 2018 Safeguarding Summit, where the United Nations, international financial institutions, multilateral development banks, nongovernment organizations, private sector suppliers, research funders, CDC Group, global funds, and the International Federation of Red Cross and Red Crescent Societies all made commitments to prevent, mitigate, and respond to SEAH.

[a] D. Spencer. 2018. *Cowboys and Conquering Kings: Sexual Harassment, Exploitation, and Abuse in the Aid Sector*; and M. Kanetake. 2012. *UN Zero Tolerance Policy's Whereabouts: On the Discordance between Politics and Law on the Internal-External Divide*. The Amsterdam LF. 44 (4), pp. 51–61.

[b] D. Spencer. 2018. *Cowboys and Conquering Kings: Sexual Harassment, Exploitation, and Abuse in the Aid Sector*; and D. Otto. 2007. Making Sense of Zero Tolerance Policies in Peacekeeping Sexual Economies. In: V. Munro and C. Stychin, eds. *Sexuality and the Law* (first edition). Abingdon: Routledge-Cavendish, pp. 259–282.

[c] See *BBC News*. 2021. Oxfam Haiti Allegations: How the Scandal Unfolded; *BBC News*. 2021. Save the Children 'let down' staff and public over harassment claims; *BBC News*. 2021. Syria conflict: Women 'sexually exploited in return for aid; and A. Mwesigwa. 2016. World Bank cancels funding for Uganda road amid sexual assault claims. *The Guardian*. 12 January.

[d] The acronym "SEA" was replaced in 2018 in the wider development assistance sector by "SEAH." The reasons behind adding "harassment" to SEA can be found in D. Spencer. 2018. *Cowboys and Conquering Kings: Sexual Harassment, Exploitation, and Abuse in the Aid Sector*.

Source: Asian Development Bank.

Understanding Sexual Exploitation, Abuse, and Harassment and Scope of the Good Practice Note

Power Differentials and Sexual Exploitation, Abuse, and Harassment

Systemic and society-wide oppressions play out and replicate in every context, and may vary and change over time and across locations. The degree of power someone has is closely linked to structural, hierarchical, and situational factors—the less power a person has, the more they are likely to be targeted for exploitation, abuse, and harassment.[6]

SEAH can be perpetrated by any person with increased power over another individual. Most often, SEAH is perpetrated against women and girls due to structural and systemic gender inequality. Most likely, men are the perpetrators of SEAH because of the same structural and gender inequality, giving privilege to men with greater power and resources. Women and girls are at increased risk of being targeted for SEAH when they face other forms of inequality that intersect with gender.

Box 4 presents a selection of data on SEAH.

BOX 4

Sexual Exploitation, Abuse, and Harassment in Figures

In East Asia and the Pacific,[a] women and girls make up 77% of trafficked persons and the most frequently detected form of exploitation among trafficked persons in these regions is sexual exploitation, making up 61% of detected cases.[b]

In India, "74% of female construction workers reported sexual harassment in the workplace."[c]

In the United Kingdom, 68% of workers with diverse sexual orientations, gender identities, and sex characteristics have experienced at least one type of sexual harassment at work and 12% of women workers with diverse sexual orientations, gender identities, and sex characteristics reported being sexually assaulted or raped at work. Two-thirds of those who were harassed did not report it, and one in four of those who did not report the harassment felt they were silenced by fear of outing themselves.[d]

continued on next page

---

6   This section is adapted from Resource and Support Hub. 2021. *Understanding SEAH and GBV*. UK Aid: London.

> **BOX 4** *continued*
>
> In "Australia, 89% of women with disabilities and 68% of men with disabilities have experienced sexual harassment. People with disabilities are more likely than those without to have been sexually harassed in the workplace (44% and 32% respectively)."[e]
>
> In India, 87% of people with disabilities work in the informal sector, where they may be at increased risk of sexual exploitation, abuse, and harassment because of the precarious nature of their employment.[f]
>
> ---
>
> [a] East Asia and the Pacific are defined in the source literature as comprising Australia; Cambodia; Fiji; Indonesia; Japan; Malaysia; the Marshall Islands; Mongolia; the People's Republic of China; the Philippines; the Republic of Korea; Solomon Islands; Taipei,China; Thailand; and Viet Nam.
> [b] UN Women, Asia and the Pacific. *Facts and Figures: Ending Violence Against Women and Girls.*
> [c] A. Rai and A. Sarkar. 2012. Workplace Culture & Status of Women Construction Labourers: a case study in Kolkata, West Bengal *Indian Journal of Spatial Science.* 1(2).
> [d] Trades Union Congress (TUC). 2019. *Sexual Harassment of LGBT People in the Workplace: A TUC Report.* https://www.tuc.org.uk/sites/default/files/LGBT_Sexual_Harassment_Report_0.pdf.
> [e] Australian Human Rights Commission. 2018. *Everyone's Business: Fourth National Survey on Sexual Harassment in Australian Workplaces* (fourth edition).
> [f] M. Shenoy. 2011. *Persons with Disability and the India Labour Market: Challenges and Opportunities.* Geneva: International Labour Organization.
>
> Source: Asian Development Bank.

Children- and Adults-at-Risk

In addition to gender, age and disability are important power differentials to consider in addressing SEAH. Children (boys and girls), particularly children with disabilities,[7] are at significantly increased risk of being targeted for sexual abuse. People with disabilities that limit communication and cognition are at very high risk of being targeted for SEAH. They may not be able to provide informed consent, may not be able to report abuse (where there is not an accessible means of reporting), or there may be stigma and harmful social norms within their community toward people with disabilities that leave them isolated in situations of higher risk (for example, unable to find work, or being in separate education facilities).

For this GPN, and in line with the United Nations Convention on the Rights of the Child,[8] anyone under the age of 18 is to be considered a child, unless under the law applicable to the child, majority is attained earlier. Children are unable to provide informed consent to sexual activity as they are still developing the cognitive, behavioral, and emotional faculties needed to fully assess the future consequences of their actions.[9] It is recommended that sex with anyone with a cognitive disability who is unable to provide informed consent as an adult should be similarly prohibited by the codes of conduct of executing and implementing agencies and contractors.

---

[7] Save the Children UK. 2011. *Out from the Shadows: Sexual Violence Against Children with Disabilities.* London.
[8] United Nations Children's Fund (UNICEF) UK. 2021. *What Is the UN Convention on Child Rights?*
[9] World Health Organization (WHO). 2017. *Responding to children and adolescents who have been sexually abused: WHO clinical guidelines.* Geneva. https://apps.who.int/iris/bitstream/handle/10665/259270/9789241550147-eng.pdf.

Understanding Informed Consent

Consent to sexual acts must always be "informed." This means that an individual must have all relevant facts at the time consent is given. There is no consent when agreement is obtained through coercion, abduction, fraud, manipulation, deception, or misrepresentation. A child or person with a cognitive disability may be unable to provide informed consent as an adult.[10]

Understanding informed consent is very important and is often an issue raised when training individuals on addressing SEAH. Box 5 answers some frequently asked questions.

BOX 5
Good to Know

Can sexual exploitation appear to be consensual? Sexual exploitation can occur in relationships that appear to be consensual. Both parties may consent, but a sexually exploitative relationship is characterized by an unequal power relationship because of power differentials (such as gaps in social status or income) between sexual partners.

Is buying sex a form of sexual exploitation? While prostitution is legal in some countries, the Asian Development Bank is committed to supporting developing member countries' efforts to end the sexual exploitation of women and children, such as soliciting, curb crawling, owning or managing a brothel, prostitution dens, child prostitution, pimping, pandering, and all forms of human trafficking.

Does sexual harassment only happen in the workplace? Sexual harassment can occur anywhere. For example, in work, before and after work, within training environments, in public spaces, and online. It can be committed by someone who has authority over another, by a peer, or even by a subordinate. It may also happen between strangers, as in the case of street and public place harassment.

Source: Asian Development Bank.

Scope of the Good Practice Note

This GPN covers the following:

✅ The prevention, mitigation, and response to SEAH perpetrated by consultants, contractors, and subcontractors who are engaged by executing or implementing agencies to work on ADB-financed sovereign projects with civil works.

✅ Good practice to prevent, mitigate, and respond to SEAH within ADB-financed sovereign projects with civil works. This GPN is intended to support ADB staff, executing and implementing agency staff, consultants, and contractors in designing measures to address SEAH during the pilot phase in selected DMCs.

---

[10] World Bank. 2020. *Addressing Sexual Exploitation and Abuse and Sexual Harassment (SEA/SH) in Investment Project Financing Involving Major Civil Works* (Second edition). Washington, DC.

This GPN does not cover the following:

❌ SEAH perpetrated by ADB personnel.[11] This is covered by ADB's Code of Conduct,[12] the Board Code of Conduct, and the Standards of Conduct, as applicable. ADB's Code of Conduct provides its staff members and other covered persons[13] with instruction on adhering to the highest standards of integrity, and ethical and respectful conduct. It also supports the right of staff to work in an environment free from inappropriate behavior, misconduct, harassment (including sexual harassment), and bullying.

❌ Incidents, issues, or concerns where the subject of concern is not an ADB-financed project worker.[14]

❌ SEAH perpetrated by executing and/or implementing agency personnel whose position is not paid for by ADB funds.

---

[11] ADB personnel includes members of ADB's Board of Directors, staff, and direct-hire consultants and contractors.

[12] ADB. 2020. Code of Conduct. Administrative Orders. AO 2.02. Manila.

[13] Specifically: (a) all ADB staff members; (b) any person who has signed a letter of appointment or other agreement to join ADB, even though they would not join ADB until the start date. In such case, the Code of Conduct becomes applicable to such person from the signing date and they shall comply with the relevant provisions thereof, failing which the Director General, Budget, People and Management Systems Department may impose disciplinary measures, including revocation of such appointment or agreement or other measure deemed by the Director General, Budget, People and Management Systems Department to be appropriate in the circumstances; (c) former ADB staff members with respect to (i) actions or omissions occurring on or after such person's start date or while such person was a member of the staff or (ii) any provision of the Code of Conduct that purports to apply following such person's resignation, retirement, or termination of employment with ADB; and (d) all persons whose letter of appointment, contract, renewal, or other agreement provides that such person shall be required to comply with the Code of Conduct or any part thereof.

[14] Where the perpetrator is a member of the affected community but not employed by a contractor working on an ADB-financed project.

Links to ADB's Operational Objectives and Policies

Safeguard Policy Statement. ADB's Safeguard Policy Statement (2009) considers safeguards to be understood as seeking "to avoid, minimize, or mitigate adverse environmental and social impacts, including protecting the rights of those likely to be affected or marginalized by the development process."[15] The safeguard policy's Safeguard Requirement 1: Environment sets out ADB's commitment to occupational health and safety, and to community health and safety.[16] SEAH and gender-based violence (GBV) are detrimental to occupational and community health and safety. The safeguard policy's Safeguard Requirement 2: Involuntary Resettlement and Safeguard Requirement 3: Indigenous Peoples set out the requirements to adequately respond to the needs of vulnerable groups and individuals.[17] As described in this section of the GPN, the root causes of SEAH lie within a framework of inequalities that heighten vulnerabilities. In addition, Table 1 (p. 19) highlights the increased risk of SEAH being perpetrated against people who are being relocated, resettled, or have their livelihood affected.

Gender and Development Policy and Social Protection Strategy. Para. 87 of ADB's Gender and Development Policy describes ADB's vision to do good by investing in gender equality more widely and addressing "female-focused violence" specifically.[18] Other ADB strategies, such as the Social Protection Strategy, indirectly address many of the risk factors that make some groups more vulnerable to SEAH, such as poverty, disability, and unemployment.[19]

Strategy 2030. ADB's long-term strategy prioritizes accelerating gender equality as one of seven operational priorities and further acknowledges that achieving gender equality is necessary to achieve ADB's other strategic objectives.[20] ADB's Strategy 2030 Operational Plan for Priority Two: Accelerating Progress Gender in Gender Equality, 2019–2024 states that ADB will meet this strategic objective through five key pillars: increasing women's economic empowerment, enhancing gender equality in human development, enhancing gender equality in decision-making and leadership, reducing women's time poverty and drudgery, and strengthening women's resilience to external shocks.[21] In addition, it refers to assessment of project risks of SEAH in the context of measures to eliminate GBV.[22]

---

[15] ADB. 2009. *Safeguard Policy Statement*. Manila. Safeguards are assurance measures to do no harm.
[16] Footnote 15, Appendix 1, paras. 40–44.
[17] Footnote 16, Appendix 2, paras. 15 and 16; and Appendix 3, para. 10.
[18] ADB. 2003. *Gender and Development*. Manila.
[19] ADB. 2003. *Social Protection*. Manila.
[20] ADB. 2018. *Strategy 2030: Achieving a Prosperous, Inclusive, Resilient, and Sustainable Asia and the Pacific*. Manila.
[21] ADB. 2019. *Strategy 2030 Operational Plan for Priority 2: Accelerating Progress in Gender Equality, 2019–2024*. Manila.
[22] Footnote 20, para. 41.

Sustainable Development Goal 5. Opportunities to deliver this work also include a crosscutting focus on a transformative gender equality agenda in line with Sustainable Development Goal (SDG) on gender equality.[23] Work on SDG 5 has an explicit link to the primary prevention of SEAH as it challenges gender inequality.

---

[23] SDG gender equality targets include equal access to productive and economic resources; elimination of all forms of violence against all women and girls in the public and private spheres, including trafficking and sexual and other types of exploitation; recognition and valuing unpaid care and domestic work; and enhancing the use of enabling technology, in particular information and communication technology, to promote the empowerment of women.

General Principles

Addressing SEAH is a core building block in creating prosperous and inclusive societies. While SEAH exists in all societies, it is widely underreported due to sensitivities, stigma, social norms, and lack of access to safe reporting mechanisms and legal systems, and is therefore often underestimated.

In line with global good practice, ADB operations must work under the assumption that SEAH exists in any community regardless of whether there is reporting data to support it. An absence of data and information in any context should not be construed as indicating low levels or low risk of SEAH.

Prevention, mitigation, and response to SEAH are based on the following general principles:

Principle 1: Zero tolerance to inaction on sexual exploitation, abuse, and harassment.

- ⮑ SEAH is not acceptable under any circumstance.
- ⮑ Action should be taken on every allegation.
- ⮑ Action should be fair, timely, and have due regard for procedural fairness.
- ⮑ ADB is committed to work with and support executing and implementing agencies, and partner institutions to address SEAH in the ADB-financed pilot projects.

Principle 2: Everyone has a responsibility to address sexual exploitation, abuse, and harassment.

- ⮑ Collaboration and commitment among ADB staff, consultants, and contractors, and executing and implementing agency staff are required to address SEAH.
- ⮑ ADB commits to ensuring that ADB staff, consultants, and contractors, and executing and implementing agency staff understand good practice in addressing SEAH within ADB operations.

Principle 3: Survivors are prioritized.

- Above all else, the needs, rights, and safety of survivors of SEAH should be prioritized.

- Apply a survivor-centered[24] and survivor-informed approach throughout all SEAH work (prevention, mitigation, and response).

- Respond confidentially, safely, without discrimination, and avoid causing harm.

Principle 4: Intervene as early as possible.

- Identify SEAH risks as early as possible at the project preparation stage.

- Identify projects in which SEAH incidents are more likely to take place.

- Ensure that SEAH prevention, mitigation, and response measures are resourced through the allocations of both human and financial resources.

Principle 5: Be aware of the context.

- SEAH manifests differently across countries, sectors, and projects and therefore the prevention, mitigation, and response to SEAH should be specific to the particular context.

- Consult with local populations, including populations who are at increased risk of being targeted for SEAH.

Principle 6: Be informed by gender, power, and social inclusion.

- Any approach to prevent, mitigate, and respond to SEAH must be informed by a thorough understanding of power and the ways in which power can be abused, with particular emphasis on SEAH.

Principle 7: Be proportionate.

- Design of prevention, mitigation, and response measures should be proportionate to the level of SEAH risks associated with the ADB-financed project, existing GBV and SEAH country-level national policies and frameworks and their implementation, and frameworks already in place in executing and implementing agencies to mitigate and respond to SEAH cases if they are to be reported.

---

24   See Annex A for further information.

Addressing Sexual Exploitation, Abuse, and Harassment in Project Preparation and Implementation

This section sets out how ADB will support executing and implementing agencies and contractors during the pilot implementation of this GPN. While this GPN is intended to be used as guidance in selected DMCs on a pilot basis, ADB-financed projects in other countries may also elect to implement some or all of the guidance.

This section also sets out minimum good practice standards (MGPS) based on those used by other financial institutions, the private sector, and civil society (Table 2 on p. 23 and Annex B).[25] During the piloting of this GPN, executing and implementing agencies can use the MGPS to assess contractors' and consultants' capacity to deliver robust prevention, mitigation, and response to SEAH in their operations related to ADB-financed projects. The executing and implementing agencies carry the responsibility for incorporating and monitoring of SEAH prevention, mitigation, and response measures in ADB-financed projects; while contractors are ultimately responsible for preventing, mitigating, and responding to SEAH risks for communities and workers. This section details the actions during project preparation and implementation and recommends tools that can be used. Annex C summarizes the recommended actions.

---

[25] The MGPS in this GPN have been adapted from Government of the United Kingdom, the Foreign, Commonwealth and Development Office. 2021. *Enhanced Due Diligence: SEAH for External Partners*. London.

1
PROJECT PREPARATION

The project preparation phase lays the foundation for the project. Figure 1 provides an overview of the different actions for addressing SEAH in project preparation.

Figure 1: At a Glance—Addressing Sexual Exploitation, Abuse, and Harassment in Project Preparation

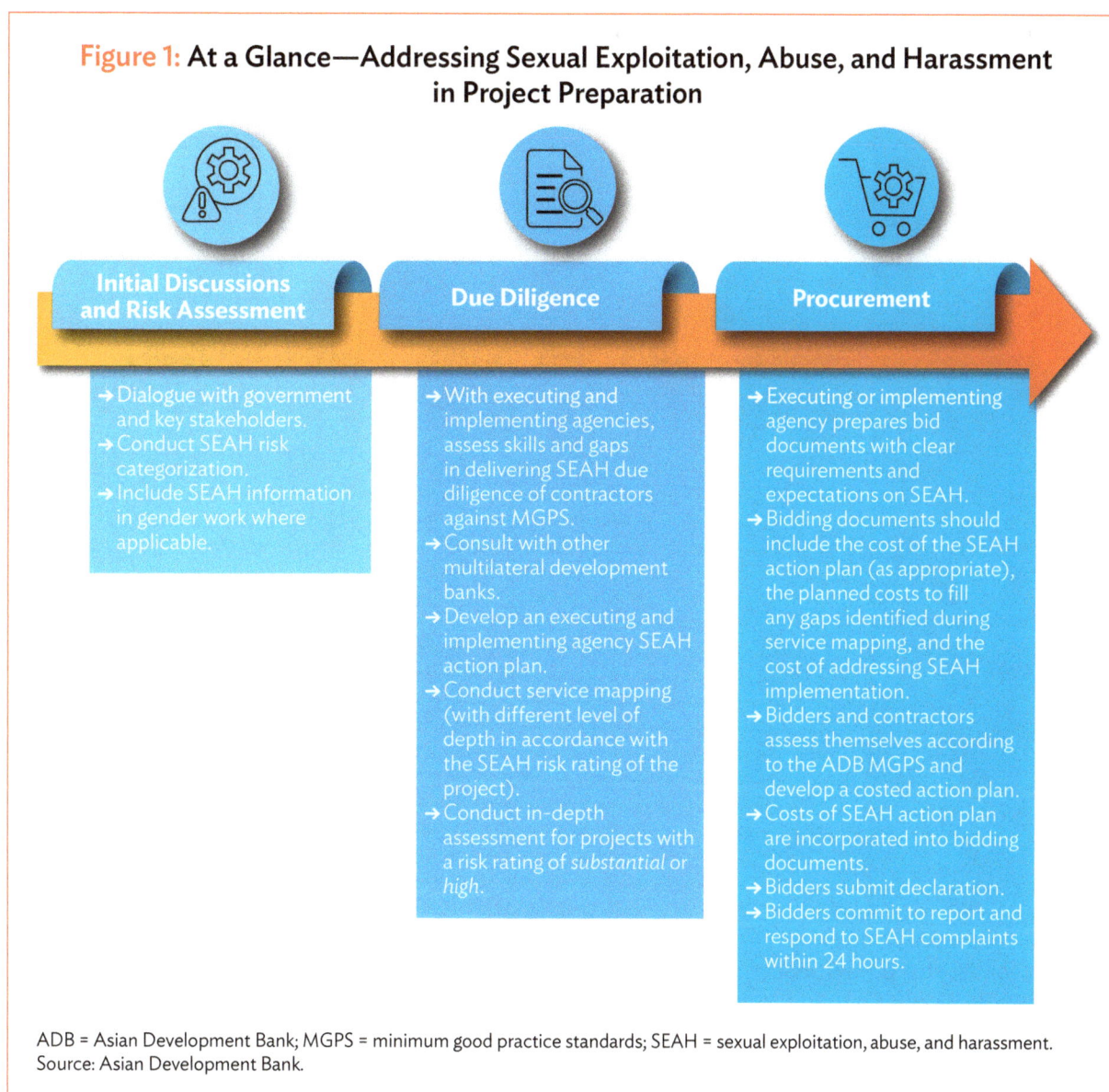

Initial Discussions and Risk Assessment	Due Diligence	Procurement
→ Dialogue with government and key stakeholders. → Conduct SEAH risk categorization. → Include SEAH information in gender work where applicable.	→ With executing and implementing agencies, assess skills and gaps in delivering SEAH due diligence of contractors against MGPS. → Consult with other multilateral development banks. → Develop an executing and implementing agency SEAH action plan. → Conduct service mapping (with different level of depth in accordance with the SEAH risk rating of the project). → Conduct in-depth assessment for projects with a risk rating of *substantial* or *high*.	→ Executing or implementing agency prepares bid documents with clear requirements and expectations on SEAH. → Bidding documents should include the cost of the SEAH action plan (as appropriate), the planned costs to fill any gaps identified during service mapping, and the cost of addressing SEAH implementation. → Bidders and contractors assess themselves according to the ADB MGPS and develop a costed action plan. → Costs of SEAH action plan are incorporated into bidding documents. → Bidders submit declaration. → Bidders commit to report and respond to SEAH complaints within 24 hours.

ADB = Asian Development Bank; MGPS = minimum good practice standards; SEAH = sexual exploitation, abuse, and harassment.
Source: Asian Development Bank.

1.   Initial Discussions with Stakeholders and Sexual Exploitation, Abuse, and Harassment Risk Assessment

a. Dialogue with Government and Key Stakeholders at National and Project Levels

During initial discussions, it is important to communicate ADB's intent to prevent, mitigate, and respond to SEAH and to support government counterparts and other key stakeholders in this aspect of project design and implementation. ADB, government counterparts, and other key stakeholders should hold initial conversations to explore the potential risks involved in the project design and ways to mitigate those risks.

At the national or regional levels or within the target sites of the project, government counterparts can share with ADB any research or other data regarding GBV and SEAH. The executing and/or implementing agencies may already have gender champions or initiatives to prevent, mitigate, and respond to SEAH—particularly where SEAH-related national legal frameworks are in place. At this stage, ADB needs to link with key government stakeholders—for example, where SEAH or gender champions exist within executing and/or implementing agency departments. Moreover, information from government counterparts may be added progressively. The following checklist summarizes the SEAH considerations to be discussed with the executing and/or implementing agencies by the ADB project team.

✓ Discuss with executing and implementing agencies the contents and scope of this GPN.

✓ Explain MGPS on SEAH and what is expected of contractors and executing and implementing agencies.

✓ Introduce the SEAH-related process outlined in this section of the GPN.

✓ Identify and agree on collaborative engagement to prevent, mitigate, and respond to SEAH risks and incidents arising in the ADB-financed projects with civil works.

✓ Highlight recommended provisions in standard bidding documents in relation to SEAH.

✓ Emphasize the respective roles and responsibilities in addressing SEAH in projects with civil works.

b. Sexual Exploitation, Abuse, and Harassment Risk Categorization of the Proposed Project

The ADB project team should complete the SEAH risk categorization of the proposed project concurrently with the environmental and social safeguards screening assessments and/or initial poverty, social, and gender assessment. The initial risk categorization should be completed as early as possible to help the project team understand the likelihood of SEAH occurring in a project. The project team will use an SEAH risk assessment tool, to generate a risk categorization through the input of country and project-specific information (Annex D*). The four project risk categories are *low*, *moderate*, *substantial*, and *high*.

Work on SEAH in subsequent phases of the project cycle will differ depending on the risk categorization of the project. For example, projects categorized as substantial or high-risk could require greater due diligence from contractors than low-risk projects. This approach is critical to ensure that the prevention, mitigation, and response measures to address SEAH in projects with civil works remain proportionate.

As part of the risk categorization process, it is important to reach out to and have meaningful consultations with civil society and government stakeholders working for women's rights, GBV response services, child protection services, and organizations working with other at-risk groups.

* Active link to Annex D SEAH Risk Assessment Tool is accessible to ADB staff and consultants.

Estimating SEAH risk is not an exact science. The risk assessment tool is meant to support the categorization of a project and to guide the ADB project team and the executing and implementing agencies on how to manage SEAH risk proportionately. Although the risk assessment tool is designed to support the process of assessing project-specific SEAH risks, there may occasionally be projects where it is more practical to adopt a higher risk category if local conditions warrant (for example, where there are likely to be higher levels of sexual violence in a specific context than has been recorded at the national level).

Table 1 introduces some of the SEAH risk factors that are applicable to projects with civil works financed by multilateral development banks (MDBs).[26] These examples are illustrative and inexhaustive. SEAH-related risks may change over time and across locations, and it is crucial to continuously monitor the situation throughout the lifetime of the project. The risks in Table 1 are captured in the risk assessment tool. The table outlines why it is important to factor these risks into the project risk assessment.

Table 1: Sexual Exploitation, Abuse, and Harassment Risk Factors and Explanations

	Risk Factor	Explanation
Country Context	1. **Rate of intimate partner violence (IPV) is high.**	Sexual exploitation, abuse, and harassment (SEAH) is rooted in gender-based violence (GBV). Therefore, when IPV is high, other forms of GBV (including SEAH) are likely to be high. However, it should also be noted that a country with higher reporting rates of IPV may not have a higher number of incidents compared with a country with lower reporting rates; it may instead have trusted and effective reporting mechanisms and a trained and supportive legal system. Reporting rates are not the same as prevalence.
	2. **Rate of non-partner sexual violence is high.**	SEAH is a form of non-partner sexual violence. Although data on non-partner sexual violence often exclude harassment and other forms of non-criminalized sexual assault, official figures are often a good indicator of the acceptance of SEAH. As in risk factor 1, the reported rates of non-partner sexual violence should not be equated with prevalence but can be used to guide risk.
	3. **Rate of child marriage is high.**	Child marriage rates can provide indicators of SEAH. The age of marriage is often linked to the age of consent to sexual activity. Child marriage is also an indicator of the acceptance of sex with a child, the parameters of bodily autonomy for women and girls, the risk of IPV, and levels of education for women and girls, which are all factors that exacerbate the risk of SEAH.
	4. **Legal framework toward women's rights is discriminatory.**	In contexts where national and local laws do not address all forms of GBV, and/or there is poor or dangerous enforcement, there is a high probability that these forms of violence are widespread and underreported. There is a need to review the legal framework concerning GBV, with reference to other parts of the legal framework that may contribute to lower reporting and heightened levels of impunity, such as discrimination within the family, restricted bodily integrity and autonomy, restricted access to productive and financial resources, and restricted civil liberties.

continued on next page

---

[26] S. Neville et al. 2020. *Addressing Gender-Based Violence and Harassment Emerging Good Practice Note for the Private Sector*, European Bank for Reconstruction and Development, the International Finance Corporation, and CDC; World Bank. 2020. *Good Practice Note on Addressing Sexual Exploitation and Abuse and Sexual Harassment (SEA/SH) in Investment Project Financing involving Major Civil Works* (second edition). Washington, DC; and ICED. 2019. *Sexual exploitation, abuse, and harassment (SEAH) Infrastructure Tool*. Department for International Development of the United Kingdom. London.

Table 1 *continued*

	Risk Factor	Explanation
Country Context	5. **Human rights rating is poor (an indicator of the treatment of marginalized groups).**	Inequalities can lead to power imbalances, which increase people's vulnerabilities to SEAH. They can also limit people's access to means to report SEAH and seek support. For example, where women do not have access to justice following sexual abuse, this may increase impunity; and where it is illegal to be homosexual, this may increase opportunities for the sexual exploitation of a person based on their sexual orientation.
	6. **Project implementation will be in humanitarian crisis-affected contexts (environmental or conflict).**	In fragile or conflict-affected contexts or where humanitarian aid is being delivered, laws that prevent and respond to SEAH are less likely to be implemented effectively. This can reduce reporting and increase the risk of impunity for perpetrators.
	7. **Project will be implemented in isolated locations.**	Remote locations can make it difficult for workers and community members to report SEAH and access support services. This can reduce reporting and increase the risk of impunity for perpetrators.
Key Informant Interviews	8. **Key informant interviews with local stakeholders suggest the incidence of GBV in the area, especially sexual violence, is substantial.**	SEAH is rooted in GBV, and therefore when GBV is high, other forms of GBV (including SEAH) are likely to be high. Desk-based information often captures reporting rates rather than prevalence (which is very difficult to capture). Gathering this information in addition to the information gathered on the country context provides a fuller understanding of GBV risk within the project's site locations. The importance of context-specific information gathered from key informants is given due consideration in the risk rating weighting calculation.
	9. **Key informant interviews with local stakeholders suggest a likelihood of SEAH occurring as a result of the proposed project or program.**	Key informants should be asked to identify risks associated with the project. Although risk associated with the project is covered elsewhere in the risk assessment tool, key informants will be able to provide guidance on context-specific risk factors, which might otherwise not be considered. To better understand SEAH risks, see Annex E for illustrative examples of the ways in which SEAH may manifest in key sectors of Asian Development Bank operations. It is important to note that risks are specific to the context, project, and contract design and the list in Annex E is not exhaustive.
	10. **Key informant interviews indicate inadequacy of appropriate SEAH response services in the project area.**	Key informants will be able to provide an overall understanding of the response services available within the project site. Supplementary information will be gathered during the executing and/or implementing agencies' service mapping; however, this indicator of risk will provide enough information for initial risk categorization.
Project Design	11. **Project is a category A or B for involuntary resettlement impacts.**[a]	Displacement of local populations can result in increased risks for marginalized populations, including risks of SEAH perpetrated by those managing the land acquisition. For example, discriminatory compensation processes may result in increased SEAH risks.
	12. **Project is a category A or B for indigenous peoples impacts.**[b]	Where the contractor's personnel may have direct contact with indigenous populations, the potential risks of SEAH increase.
	13. **There is potential for involvement of military or private security forces in the project.**	Security guards are in a position of power in relation to the community, especially women and girls. They can abuse this position. It is therefore critical that when security personnel are employed, this is done using robust recruitment processes to select, train, manage, and monitor the behavior of security companies and their personnel. The military can take on an authority role, even when they are not contracted as part of the project. It is critical to have an understanding with the executing and implementing agencies on how to handle such a situation.
	14. **Project implementation will be primarily through third-party contractors such as subcontractors, suppliers, or sub-consultants.**	Complex supply chains and extensive use of third-party contractors, suppliers, and/or consultants can make it more difficult to ensure effective oversight of all those involved to prevent, mitigate, and respond to SEAH.

continued on next page

Table 1 *continued*

	Risk Factor	Explanation
Project Implementation	15. The project will be working directly with or in the vicinity of a school or any other places that children frequent.	Children are at increased risk of SEAH being perpetrated against them where there is an increase in their interaction with unknown adults. This is because of the difference in power between a child and an adult.
	16. The project will operate close to places frequented by women, indigenous people, ethnic minorities, or other discriminated against groups.	There may also be increased risk of SEAH taking place where ADB projects are implemented within a 5-minute walk of a reproductive health care clinic, an HIV testing center, or a community center working with any other groups facing discrimination.
	17. The project will lead to a large influx of male workers from other regions within the country.	During construction, workers are often employed informally, are predominantly male, often stay at project construction sites for only short periods of time, and often come without their families. This can increase the risk of SEAH.
	18. Project will lead to a large influx of male workers from outside the country.	There is an increased risk where large numbers of men employed are from a context with different social norms concerning women's rights (international workers, for example). The risk of SEAH increasing in such a context will depend on the size of the workforce. Continuous feedback from women, girls, and other groups that are discriminated against during project implementation is critical.
	19. The project will be implemented in a large geographic area and with a large population affected.	It may be more difficult to ensure proper awareness-raising and monitoring of implementation if the project is large and spread across a large geographic area.
Project Workforce	20. The project will employ women primarily to hold more junior or less formal positions.	Where women primarily occupy low-level jobs with male supervisors, the risk of SEAH increases, including in relation to sexual harassment and withholding wages and/or promotions in return for sexual favors.
	21. There is potential for local women to be working in the construction camps with predominantly foreign construction workers.	During construction, workers are often employed informally, are predominantly male, often stay at project construction sites for only short periods of time, and often come without their families. This can increase the risk of SEAH. There is an increased risk where large numbers of men employed are from a context with different social norms concerning women's rights (international workers, for example).
	22. There is potential for local women to be working in the construction camps with predominantly migrant construction workers from the same country.	The risk of SEAH increasing in such a context will depend on the size of the workforce. Continuous feedback from women, girls, and other groups that are discriminated against during project implementation is critical.
	23. There may be challenges in ensuring that all the staff and contractors hired by the executing and/or implementing agencies and any contractors and subcontractors working on the project sign codes of conduct prohibiting them from engaging in SEAH.	Where clear codes of conduct, policies, practices, and procedures are not in place and understood by all those working on projects and/or are not well communicated, SEAH can flourish as staff are unaware of the expected standards of behavior, reporting mechanism, or protocols for preventing SEAH, mitigating SEAH, and handling incidents.
	24. There may be challenges in ensuring proper training and awareness-raising among all construction employees on zero tolerance to GBV and SEAH and penalties.	

[a] Category A projects are likely to have significant involuntary resettlement impacts. Category B projects include involuntary resettlement impacts that are not deemed significant. (ADB. 2009. *Safeguard Policy Statement*. Manila. https://www.adb.org/documents/safeguard-policy-statement).

[b] Category A projects are likely to have significant impacts on indigenous peoples. Category B projects are likely to have limited impacts on indigenous peoples. (ADB. 2009. *Safeguard Policy Statement*. Manila. https://www.adb.org/documents/safeguard-policy-statement).

Source: Asian Development Bank.

c. Inclusion of Sexual Exploitation, Abuse, and Harassment in Gender Work

ADB's initial project gender categorization provides an entry point to think about how to further enhance and strengthen systems, policies, and practices to prevent, mitigate, and respond to SEAH. Projects categorized gender equity theme or effective gender mainstreaming[27] embark on gender work that entails the preparation of gender action plans in which proactive gender designs to address potential GBV and SEAH risks can be added above and beyond the project's "do-no-harm" measures. This may include helping develop institutional SEAH policies and response protocols for executing and/or implementing agencies or strengthening the capacity of service providers and government stakeholders to prevent, mitigate, and respond to SEAH risks. Close coordination between SEAH specialists and gender and development specialists can be useful.

2. Support Executing and Implementing Agencies during Due Diligence

SEAH due diligence work in the pilot projects centers on understanding whether the executing and/or implementing agency needs support to deliver SEAH-related due diligence of consultants and contractors and monitor consultants' and contractors' adherence to the MGPS. During this stage, the executing and/or implementing agency should put in place an SEAH action plan that considers the resources and time needed to fill any gaps in the agency's capacity to conduct their due diligence process with contractors against the MGPS.

a. Work with Executing and Implementing Agencies to Assess Their Skills and Gaps in Delivering Due Diligence of Contractors

During this phase, the ADB project team can support and work in partnership with the executing and/or implementing agency to review the MGPS and assess what they need to (i) deliver the effective due diligence of contractors; (ii) monitor the implementation of the MGPS by consultants, contractors, and subcontractors; and (iii) put in place provisions for the appropriate setup and oversight of response mechanisms.

It is important that the executing and/or implementing agency's due diligence process for contractors takes place early in the procurement phase. Executing and implementing agencies should ensure they have the skills to adequately engage in the SEAH-focused due diligence process. It is recommended that projects with civil works go through the due diligence process irrespective of whether the contracting is to be carried out under advance procurement or during project implementation. During this phase, contractors should provide evidence to the executing and/or implementing agencies that they can meet the MGPS. Contractors may also be asked to demonstrate how they will monitor and report SEAH compliance by their subcontractors to the executing and/or implementing agencies.

The capacity of executing and/or implementing agencies to deliver due diligence in accordance with the MGPS will be reviewed through a self-assessment tool (Annex F-1) and through reflective conversations with the ADB project team. The risk rating of the project should determine the depth of this review.

---

[27] ADB. 2021. *Guidelines for Gender Mainstreaming Categories of ADB Projects*. Manila.

The self-assessment tool for contractors is in Annex G-1. For projects rated low and moderate risk, the contractor's due diligence review process should focus on compliance. The executing and/or implementing agency's review should determine whether the contractor has the necessary policies, practices, and procedures in place. For projects rated substantial- and high-risk, the in-depth review should focus on compliance and the content of policies, practices, and procedures that are in place and will be used by the contractor to mitigate SEAH risks and respond to SEAH cases.

It is critical that the executing and implementing agencies have a clear understanding of what it would take to implement each of the standards of the SEAH MGPS, including the needs assessment for expertise to review materials and assess SEAH action plans proposed by contractors. Annex F contains a sample template for an SEAH action plan and the self-assessment tool for executing and implementing agencies. A sample of the code of conduct—a priority standard of the MGPS—is in Annex H.

Areas A, B, C, E, and H in the MGPS are priority standards (Table 2),[28] and it is important for executing and/or implementing agencies to emphasize these actions when reviewing the proposed SEAH action plans by contractors. It is prudent to advise on delaying implementation until the contractors can meet these priority standards, especially in projects rated substantial- and high-risk.

Table 2: Sexual Exploitation, Abuse, and Harassment Minimum Good Practice Standards for Contractors

Executing and implementing agencies should be able to ensure that contractors have the following in place as a minimum.

Area	Minimum Good Practice Standard for Contractors
A. **SEAH policy** (Priority standard)	1. Have a policy or combination of policies that address SEAH in the workplace and in the community.
B. **Code of conduct** (Priority standard)	2. Have a clear employee code of conduct that prohibits all forms of SEAH and requires regular training for all personnel.
C. **Reporting, handling of complaints, and whistleblowing** (standards 4–9 may be outsourced to an appropriate specialized partner) (Priority standards)	3. Have or be willing to develop a comprehensive and confidential SEAH reporting mechanism for escalating and managing concerns and complaints. This should include the option of anonymous reporting and whistleblowing. They must be accessible to workers, community members who come into contact with contractors' staff, and workers.
	4. Be able to work with communities and constituencies to analyze the most appropriate and accessible means to report concerns and complaints. Multiple reporting methods must be put in place.
	5. Be able to promote the code of conduct and reporting mechanisms to the staff and the community or communities in the project area.
	6. Have a clear internal handling framework (standard operating procedure) to respond appropriately to all concerns and support the survivor in a survivor-centered way.
	7. Have identified and risk-assessed services available within the project context to ensure safe referrals of survivors can take place.
	8. Have in-house trained investigators or have identified an appropriate external investigation resource.
	9. Have a whistleblowing policy that includes SEAH.

continued on next page

28 These standards are prioritized because they have the most direct impact on organizational culture, ensuring appropriate reporting and response mechanisms are in place, and impact on potential and actual survivors of SEAH.

Table 2 *continued.*

Area	Minimum Good Practice Standard for Contractors
D. Human resources	10. Ensure all staff, contractors, volunteers, and other representatives have at least mandatory induction training when they commence employment and annual refresher training on the code of conduct and the organization's SEAH policy and whistleblowing policy, or a combination of relevant policies.
	11. Have a recruitment approach that includes specific interview question(s) that draw out applicants' attitudes and values in relation to at-risk groups.
E. Risk management (Priority standards)	12. Have a comprehensive and effective risk management framework in place that includes reference to SEAH and the creation of a central register of SEAH reports.
	13. Have requirements for maintaining and updating the central register of SEAH concerns, including information confidentiality requirements.
F. Working with subcontractors and suppliers	14. Include information on SEAH risks and expectations in contracts.
	15. Review subcontractors' policies against these minimum standards or similar standards. Where subcontractors do not have policies, practices, and procedures in place, subcontractors and suppliers should adhere to the contracting agency's code of conduct.
	16. Provide information to subcontractors and suppliers about project reporting mechanisms and the need to ensure these are in place.
G. Workplace design	17. Include SEAH in regular workplace safety assessments, including working accommodation, transportation, and site safety.
H. Leadership and accountability (Priority standards)	18. Communicate regularly regarding their zero tolerance to inaction on SEAH utilizing internal and external communication routes.
	19. Have clear guidelines for monitoring and overseeing implementation of the policy or policies.
	20. Have the capacity to be able to report allegations within 24 hours to the executing and/or implementing agencies.

SEAH = sexual exploitation, abuse, and harassment.
Source: Asian Development Bank.

b. Consult with Other Multilateral Development Banks

During project preparation, the executing and/or implementing agencies will demonstrate their willingness and ability to put in place accountability and quality assurance mechanisms to monitor the contractors' response to SEAH. It may be practical to consult with other MDBs and international financial institutions to assess systems and practices already in place and develop coordinated SEAH action plan measures without overlapping to avoid duplication.

c. Develop Executing and Implementing Agency Sexual Exploitation, Abuse, and Harassment Action Plan

At this stage, the executing and/or implementing agencies can develop a costed SEAH action plan with prioritized actions for completion within the first year of the project. Ideally, the action plan should include the capacity development of executing and/or implementing agency staff involved in due diligence and the monitoring, reporting, and handling of SEAH complaints. It may also contain actions relating to service strengthening or establishing SEAH support services, if needed. The template for the SEAH action plan, including key areas for consideration based on the self-assessment, is in Annex F.

d. Conduct Service Mapping

A basic service mapping report is recommended for projects rated moderate and low risk, while an enhanced service mapping report is recommended for projects rated substantial- and high-risk (Figure 2). In any project, the lack of services is a risk factor that needs to be identified and addressed. The ability to refer SEAH survivors to safe and appropriate services is of utmost importance. Annex I contains a service mapping guide.

Figure 2: Understanding the Relationship between Risk Levels and Actions to be Taken Regarding Service Mapping

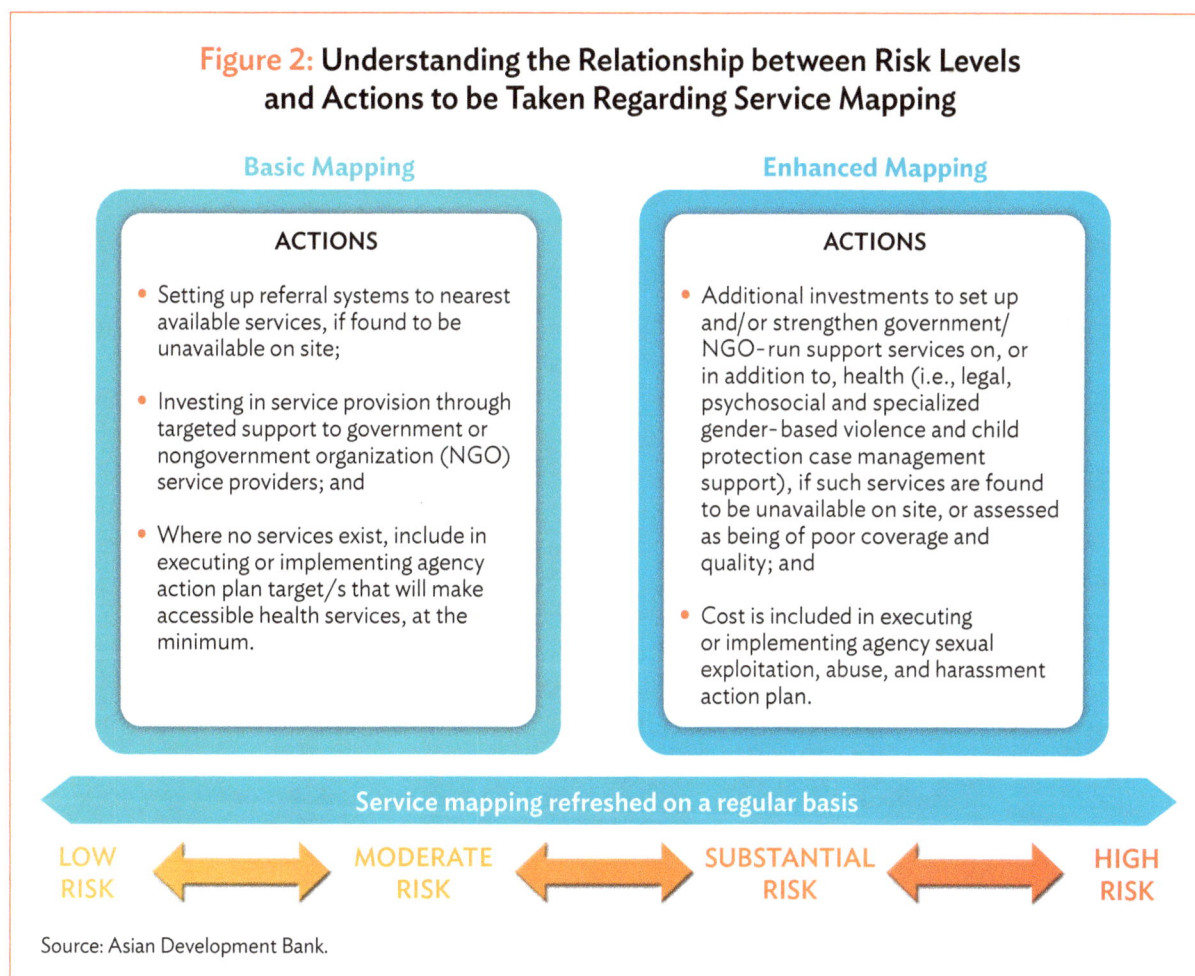

Basic Mapping

ACTIONS

- Setting up referral systems to nearest available services, if found to be unavailable on site;

- Investing in service provision through targeted support to government or nongovernment organization (NGO) service providers; and

- Where no services exist, include in executing or implementing agency action plan target/s that will make accessible health services, at the minimum.

Enhanced Mapping

ACTIONS

- Additional investments to set up and/or strengthen government/NGO-run support services on, or in addition to, health (i.e., legal, psychosocial and specialized gender-based violence and child protection case management support), if such services are found to be unavailable on site, or assessed as being of poor coverage and quality; and

- Cost is included in executing or implementing agency sexual exploitation, abuse, and harassment action plan.

Service mapping refreshed on a regular basis

| LOW RISK | | MODERATE RISK | | SUBSTANTIAL RISK | | HIGH RISK |

Source: Asian Development Bank.

All service mapping should include an assessment of the services available in the project area; their quality; who can access them (for example, whether they are inclusive of boys and girls; whether they are disability friendly; and whether they will serve people with diverse sexual orientations, gender identities, and sex characteristics); any associated cost; and the distance from the project site and communities. Some of this information can be sourced from national or local government departments and nongovernment organizations (NGOs). Executing and/or implementing agencies are encouraged to engage with existing service providers and stakeholders as much as possible. Service mapping and associated resources (such as national, or local service and referral pathways) may already be in place, particularly in humanitarian contexts, where GBV and child protection working groups can be engaged to help support mapping and the creation of referral pathways.

Where the coverage and/or quality of support services is poor, or where certain groups are considered underserved, the service mapping report should propose actions to address these gaps. This may include referring SEAH survivors to services further away (up to 4 hours of travel by car) or investing in strengthening service provision through targeted support to the government or an NGO. Where services are nonexistent, a costed plan should be drawn up to ensure that health services (at a minimum) are in place. As outlined in the mapping guide, under health, the aim should be to meet all elements of the service mapping, starting with providing clinical care for sexual assault survivors. Mapping should be used to develop the project's referral pathway and should be updated regularly throughout the project.

Where a new project is being set up in the same location as an ongoing or recently closed project, the mapping conducted and maintained during the earlier project can be used by the new project. The service mapping should be updated if it was conducted more than 12 months earlier. Sharing of mapping and referral pathways between projects should be encouraged and a common-sense approach is taken to progressively update the mapping used.

For projects with substantial and high SEAH risk and where support service coverage and/or quality are assessed as poor (i.e., not within a 4-hour car journey), additional resources should be considered to set up or strengthen services for SEAH survivors to provide health, legal, psychosocial, and specialized GBV and child protection case management support. Preference should always be given to strengthening services where they exist as this approach is more sustainable than establishing new services.

It is important to specify the costs of strengthening or establishing services where they are not available in the costed SEAH action plan of the executing and/or implementing agency. Mapping must include an assessment of the safety of services and whether they are survivor-centered.

For projects rated substantial- and high-risk, it is prudent to prepare an in-depth SEAH analysis and risk assessment report as part of due diligence. Data gathered from this assessment will inform the project SEAH action plan on how and where services may be provided if SEAH occurs. The terms of reference (TOR) for the in-depth assessment should be tailored to the context of the project and project site. Table 3 provides an overview of how to approach the assessment. The tool in Annex J, Key Guiding Questions when Reviewing a Project SEAH Analysis and Assessment Analysis, is useful for preparing TOR for engaging external consultants to deliver or review assessments.

Consultations should be conducted in line with global good practice to help potential survivors avoid experiencing stress, distress, and trauma as a result. Interviews with survivors should not knowingly take place (Box 6). Refer to Annex K for examples of data collection methods for in-depth assessments.

Table 3: Overview of Suggested Contents of In-Depth Assessment and Enhanced Service Mapping Terms of Reference

Purpose and time frame	The time frame will vary depending on the following key factors, which should be clear from information gathered during project preparation: • the size, scale, and complexity of the investment, project, or civil works, including the number and location of worksites; • the size and composition of the workforce and whether interactions with community members and service users are expected; and • the nature of the sexual exploitation, abuse, and harassment (SEAH) risks.
Skills	Specialists conducting the in-depth assessment will need to have • knowledge of the root causes of SEAH and the forms it can take; • experience in assessing, designing, and/or implementing approaches to prevent SEAH; • experience in assessing, designing, and/or implementing grievance mechanisms for workers, community members, and/or service users; and • knowledge of the project's sociocultural setting. If an SEAH expert is not available locally, it may be necessary to identify a regional or international SEAH expert to conduct the in-depth assessment of SEAH risks. SEAH experts should have experience of the country context. However, this is not essential if they are working with someone who has knowledge of the local social, political, and legal context.
Approach and methodology	Once commissioned, the SEAH expert will need to • develop a tailored methodology for the in-depth assessment; and • set out clear procedures for the SEAH expert to follow if the SEAH expert identifies an incident of SEAH during the in-depth assessment. The in-depth assessment methodology should ideally involve a desk review of existing information and data gathering in the project location.
Outputs	The outputs of the in-depth assessment of SEAH risks may include • an explanation of SEAH risks for the project; • a description of required executing and/or implementing agency capacity and resources to prevent, mitigate, and respond to SEAH; which should lead to the executing and/or implementing agency SEAH action plan being amended where necessary; • a detailed set of SEAH prevention and mitigation measures as part of the SEAH action plan to be implemented by the project, including standard operating procedures for response and case handling; and • detailed service mapping for referrals and an assessment of their safety.

Source: Adapted from S. Neville et al. 2020. *Addressing Gender-Based Violence and Harassment: Emerging Good Practice for the Private Sector*. European Bank for Reconstruction and Development, CDC, and International Finance Corporation.

BOX 6

Never Seek Out Survivors

Do not ask individuals about their experiences of sexual exploitation, abuse, and harassment (SEAH) when conducting an assessment, monitoring, research, or evaluation work.[a] It is important that efforts to identify SEAH risks do not include attempts to identify people who have experienced or witnessed SEAH, be they community members, workers, or service users. No one should be asked any direct questions about SEAH or their experiences with it. This is unnecessary and may cause harm or distress by re-traumatizing people who have survived or witnessed SEAH.

---

[a] A survivor may volunteer information, but this should not be as a result of direct or probing questions seeking for them to disclose the information.

Source: Adapted from S. Neville et al. 2020. *Addressing Gender-Based Violence and Harassment: Emerging Good Practice for the Private Sector*. European Bank for Reconstruction and Development, CDC, and International Finance Corporation.

3. Address Sexual Exploitation, Abuse, and Harassment through the Procurement Process

The procurement process requirements described in this section apply to a bidding process that may take place during project design or implementation.

a. Executing and/or Implementing Agency Prepares Bid Documents Addressing Identified Sexual Exploitation, Abuse, and Harassment Issues

The executing and/or implementing agency should include clear and comprehensive SEAH requirements and MGPS in the relevant sections of the bid documents to ensure that bidders understand these requirements, submit their bids following the requirements, and demonstrate the ability to address defined SEAH risks during contract implementation depending on the SEAH risk assessment results during project preparation. The executing and/or implementing agency will be responsible for defining the SEAH-relevant deliverables in the "employer's requirement" section of the bid document.

b. Executing and/or Implementing Agency Checks the Submission of Documents by the Bidder–Contractor

Prospective contractors submit to the executing and/or implementing agency the following documents:

(i) **Minimum good practice standard self-assessment.** Prospective bidders should submit an MGPS-based self-assessment to reveal organizational capacities and gaps in addressing SEAH concerns, should they arise.

(ii) **Action plan and budget.** Bidders need to prepare a contractor's SEAH action plan (Annex G-2) and a budget that can address the gaps identified in their MGPS self-assessment. Bidders must submit the action plan as part of their bids with the associated costs for its implementation, following the requirements of bid documents. The implementation cost of the contractor's SEAH action plan may be included in the bid documents, either built into the unit rates or as a specified provisional sum for activities whose scope and cost cannot be estimated accurately in advance. Funds to be used against a specified provisional sum should include details of activities such as awareness-raising and capacity building for employees, filling gaps in their SEAH frameworks, and meeting ADB's SEAH MGPS.[29] The bidder will determine the human resources and material facilities needed to implement the SEAH action plan. Securing specialized SEAH and/or GBV expertise and services is crucial, especially for projects categorized substantial- and high-risk. Bidders that lack the capacity to deliver the outputs may outsource the implementation of activities such as SEAH reporting and case handling; response services (counseling, shelter, investigation, protection, legal, and medical support); training; and research. The executing and/or implementing agency will examine the

---

[29] Depending on the nature and clarity of SEAH scope, a provisional sum can be defined as competitive items or a defined provisional amount to be paid on an actual basis.

relevance and soundness of the SEAH action plan and budget in relation to the bidder's MGPS self-assessment, potential SEAH issues, and gaps identified in the service mapping report.

(iii) **Code of conduct.** The bidders must submit a code of conduct with explicit SEAH requirements as set out by the employer in the bid document as part of their bid. A sample of the SEAH code of conduct with SEAH-related requirements is in Annex H. The bidder should not substantially modify the code of conduct. However, they may add requirements, as appropriate, including those addressing contract-specific SEAH issues and risks.

(iv) **Declaration on contractual issues and response to previous sexual exploitation, abuse, and harassment concerns.** Bidders must submit a declaration stating whether they have had a contract terminated or suspended or a performance security called for reasons relating to past poor performance on SEAH. Bidders that have had a contract terminated for SEAH noncompliance must demonstrate that the issue that led to termination, suspension, or performance review has been resolved. The executing and/or implementing agency is responsible for checking validity of the bidder's declaration. If ADB later learns that the contractor's declaration is false, this can form the basis for a misrepresentation allegation that becomes actionable under ADB's Integrity Principles and Guidelines.[30]

(v) **Commitment to report and respond to complaints within 24 hours.** ADB's standard bidding document template contains a respectful work environment clause.[31] In addition, bidders will be required to submit a signed commitment to report any SEAH incidents to the executing and/or implementing agency within 24 hours of receiving a report.

Additional information

✓ Special efforts are made to draw the attention of bidders to the SEAH requirements through market engagement, use of clarifications, and/or during pre-bid meetings.

✓ The bidder's documents are usually assessed on fail/pass criteria defined in the bid documents. Where appropriate, a merit point scoring system may be used to evaluate the bidder's SEAH proposal as per the requirement of the bid documents.

---

[30] ADB. 2015. *Integrity Principles and Guidelines*. Manila.
[31] ADB. 2021. *User Guide for Procurement of Works: Standard Bidding Document*. Manila.

2

PROJECT IMPLEMENTATION AND CONTRACT MANAGEMENT

This section discusses the actions of contractors, executing and/or implementing agencies, and ADB in three separate subsections (Figure 3). It follows a reading order that is representative of the responsibility for addressing SEAH in the project. Responsibility for monitoring and ensuring compliance with the SEAH MGPS lies with the executing and/or implementing agency, as implemented by contractors. Therefore, the executing and/or implementing agencies should oversee the implementation of the contractors' SEAH action plans, the strengthening of referral pathways (where necessary), and provide oversight and support in case handling.

Figure 3: At a Glance—Responsibility for Response to Sexual Exploitation, Abuse, and Harassment in Project Implementation and Contract Management

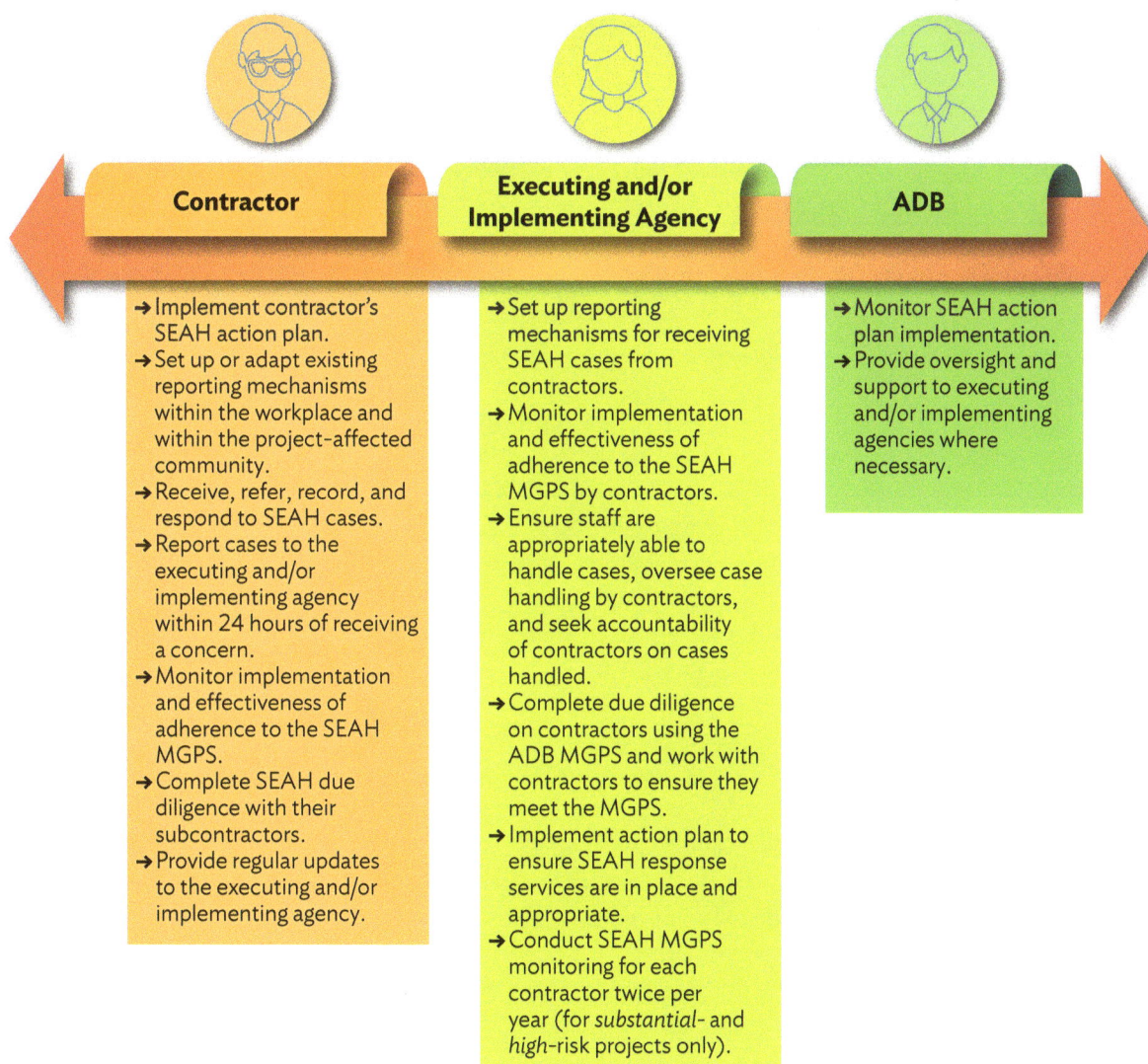

Contractor
→ Implement contractor's SEAH action plan.
→ Set up or adapt existing reporting mechanisms within the workplace and within the project-affected community.
→ Receive, refer, record, and respond to SEAH cases.
→ Report cases to the executing and/or implementing agency within 24 hours of receiving a concern.
→ Monitor implementation and effectiveness of adherence to the SEAH MGPS.
→ Complete SEAH due diligence with their subcontractors.
→ Provide regular updates to the executing and/or implementing agency.

Executing and/or Implementing Agency
→ Set up reporting mechanisms for receiving SEAH cases from contractors.
→ Monitor implementation and effectiveness of adherence to the SEAH MGPS by contractors.
→ Ensure staff are appropriately able to handle cases, oversee case handling by contractors, and seek accountability of contractors on cases handled.
→ Complete due diligence on contractors using the ADB MGPS and work with contractors to ensure they meet the MGPS.
→ Implement action plan to ensure SEAH response services are in place and appropriate.
→ Conduct SEAH MGPS monitoring for each contractor twice per year (for *substantial-* and *high-*risk projects only).

ADB
→ Monitor SEAH action plan implementation.
→ Provide oversight and support to executing and/or implementing agencies where necessary.

ADB = Asian Development Bank; MGPS = minimum good practice standards; SEAH = sexual exploitation, abuse, and harassment.
Source: Asian Development Bank.

1. Detailed Contractor Actions

Contractors are responsible for delivering the SEAH MGPS, ensuring that SEAH is prevented and mitigated and that reporting and responding to any incidents of SEAH that occur are in line with general principles and with a survivor-centered approach.

The ultimate accountability for SEAH prevention, mitigation, and response to SEAH incidents within a contractor and its operations reside with the most senior member of its staff. When the project engages construction supervision services, the engineer is responsible for ensuring that SEAH is properly addressed. The TOR of the construction supervision consultant firm should clearly outline the expectations of its role in ensuring that SEAH risks prevention, mitigation, and response measures are effectively implemented. The TOR should also include a provision for staff to be properly qualified. The contractors' actions are detailed in subsections a–g below.

a. Implement the Contractor's Sexual Exploitation, Abuse, and Harassment Action Plan

When selecting contractors for civil works, infrastructure development expertise is weighted heavily. A contract may be awarded to a qualified contractor even if all SEAH MGPS during the self-assessment exercise were not met. Any gaps in meeting the MGPS will be clarified through bid clarifications and addressed by the winning bidder through the implementation of the SEAH action plan. If the SEAH action plan was approved for funding through a provisional sum, a detailed work plan should be discussed further with the contractor during contract implementation.

Projects with substantial- and high-risk rating should prioritize preparatory activities that will contribute to ensuring contractor compliance with MGPS areas A, B, C, E, and H (Table 2). Project implementation may be delayed until these priority standards are met. These priority MGPS areas relate to organizational SEAH policies, employee code of conduct, mechanisms for reporting and handling complaints, risk management, and leadership and accountability. Contractors' SEAH action plans are most appropriate when they are phased. Setting up the mechanisms to implement the SEAH action plan should not go on for longer than a year, but the SEAH efforts should continue throughout the project life cycle.

b. Set Up or Adapt Existing Sexual Exploitation, Abuse, and Harassment Reporting Mechanisms and Establish Case Handling Protocols

All ADB-financed projects must have a grievance redress mechanism (GRM) in place. Such GRMs are set up to report and respond to a wide variety of project-related complaints, including those associated with environmental and social safeguards. Typically, project GRMs are designed to address grievances and resolve disputes regarding a negative impact brought about by the project's activities and/or individuals working on the project. However, these GRMs are not necessarily set up in a way that is suitable for receiving and handling SEAH complaints.

The key differences between a typical project GRM and one that can be used for SEAH reports are as follows:

- **Speed of response.** When a report of SEAH is received, it must be responded to within 24 hours. Reasons include, most urgently, survivors' need for lifesaving referrals to medical services.

- **Confidentiality protocols and ethical handling.** Stigmatization, rejection, and the risk of retribution and reprisals against survivors and complainants are commonplace. Where a complaints mechanism is not confidential it discourages survivors from reporting the incident. This may constrain their ability to access services through referrals and may increase the likelihood of impunity for perpetrators. Furthermore, traditional community responses to SEAH may be to push for mediation; and if the survivor is not married, communities and families may push for the survivor and the perpetrator to marry as a resolution to the issue. This puts the survivor at great risk. Where the survivor and the perpetrator are both male, there may also be associated risk in coming forward because of negative social norms concerning masculinities and sexual orientation.[32]

- **Support, not compensation.** Providing support for the survivor is the initial priority when a report is made. This means linking with mapped support services. The next priority is to ensure appropriate action is taken if the allegation is substantiated. No compensation should be provided as a part of responding to SEAH. Funds may only be used to support survivors' access to response services.

- **Multiple survivor-centered reporting mechanisms.** Reporting mechanisms should be accessible to survivors and complainants in a non-stigmatizing way. Women and girls and other at-risk populations should be meaningfully consulted to ensure multiple means of reporting are available. For example, where women and girls have low literacy, it would be important to ensure that access to reporting does not depend on being able to communicate in writing and that reporting can occur through several focal points. Where women and girls lack access to phones, a hotline may not be the most suitable means of reporting and may need to be accompanied by other reporting entry points. Conversely, a hotline may be a more suitable means of reporting for adults with diverse sexual orientation, gender identity, and sex characteristics as it could allow for non-identifying and potentially anonymous reporting of an incident or concern.

- **Availability of specific expertise.** Dealing with SEAH complaints requires specialized knowledge. It is therefore essential to recognize that without such expertise, a GRM cannot effectively deal with SEAH complaints.

It is possible to adapt or build on an existing workplace reporting mechanism or community structures for SEAH reporting. These may include the contractor's reporting mechanisms or reporting mechanisms already established by local authorities and/or NGOs or operating through other MDB projects in targeted communities. Care should be taken to ensure confidentiality and non-stigmatization in accessing these reporting mechanisms (Box 7). For example, using a physical reporting box only for SEAH reporting in a workplace may not be appropriate as those using it may be identified as survivors.

---

[32] The sexual orientation of the survivor or the subject of concern in these circumstances should not be assumed.

BOX 7

Workplace and Community Reporting Mechanisms

Separate reporting mechanisms must be set up and be accessible for both workers and community members to enable them to report sexual exploitation, abuse, and harassment (SEAH) concerns. Separate mechanisms are needed to ensure that they are suited to the access needs of each group. Multiple entry points to reporting are advisable as the needs of different groups vary. For example, women and girls may not have access to their cell phones, and therefore would not be able to access an e-mail reporting mechanism or a telephone hotline; people with disabilities may not be able to access reporting boxes set up in an inaccessible part of the project site; and in a workplace where most of the workforce have low literacy levels, an e-mail-based reporting mechanism may create a large gap in access to reporting. These access-related challenges can be avoided if reporting mechanisms are set up in consultation with at-risk groups.

An initial assessment should check whether there are local systems with which the project can engage to streamline reporting of SEAH concerns in a joint mechanism. This might include reporting mechanisms that have already been established by local authorities, nongovernment organizations, or projects of other development partners in targeted communities. Engaging women's rights groups or offering a dedicated, staffed hotline may also be options. It is important to remember that a survivor may not know where the perpetrator works and may not wish to search out the employer of the perpetrator. Shared mechanisms can reduce the barriers to SEAH reporting that some survivors face, particularly if there are many official development assistance actors working in an area.

Source: Asian Development Bank.

Table 4 provides a simple guide to setting up or strengthening an SEAH reporting mechanism.[33]

Table 4: Simple Guide to Setting Up A Reporting Mechanism

Actions	Details
Engage and consult	With • the government, local officials, and community leaders to gain buy-in and support, and to understand the context; • women, girls, and other at-risk groups within the community, working with a wide range of community groups and actors to ensure a diversity of perspectives is sought; • employees and staff members, particularly women and other at-risk staff; and • civil society organizations and women's groups. The process of creating the reporting mechanism should involve collaboration with all key actors. At-risk populations and communities affected by the project are always best placed to support the design of feedback and grievance mechanisms. The consultation process should consider power imbalances and seek to ensure that the most at-risk groups have equal access to reporting mechanisms. Engagement with communities should be done carefully. Where specific groups may not be able to talk freely in mixed groups, separate sessions may be more appropriate.

continued on next page

---

[33] Further guidance is available in the forthcoming *Good Practice Note on Integrating Sexual Exploitation, Abuse, and Harassment Reporting and Case Handling into Project Grievance Redress Mechanisms in ADB-Financed Projects with Civil Works.*

Table 4 continued.

Actions	Details
Design the reporting mechanism	• Decide whether the contractor themselves will deliver reporting and response to SEAH or whether this will be wholly or partially outsourced to a third party. This should be based on assessment against minimum good practice standards, feedback from the engagement and consultations, and the project risk assessment.
	• Ensure that reporting mechanisms are accessible to at-risk groups. Reporting mechanisms within the workplace and within the community should consider accessibility for different groups. This should be explored at length during the engagement and consultation period, and should continue to be monitored throughout the life of the project. Reporting entry points should be accessible and consider issues such as access for people with disabilities, women's access to and control of technology, and literacy levels. At least one option for anonymous reporting should be put in place.
	• Ensure that reporting mechanisms are child friendly. At least one reporting mechanism should be easily accessible to children.
	• Ensure multiple reporting entry points. Several reporting channels should be available to community members and staff.
	• Decide whether the mechanism can receive reports from suppliers and contractors as well as company workers and project-affected communities. Community members are unlikely to know the difference between one company and another delivering work on a project. Therefore, it is advisable to develop the company's reporting mechanism to receive concerns that involve workers as well as suppliers and contractors.
	• If there are many companies and/or official development assistance agencies working in the same location, it may be most appropriate to use a shared reporting mechanism with clear processes and procedures. Coordination is highly encouraged wherever possible.
Communicate	Promote key messages to the community and staff, including • what SEAH is, and that staff and community members have a right to live free from it; • the company's code of conduct; • the types of concerns and issues that can be reported through the reporting mechanism; • when, where, and how community members can access the reporting mechanism; • what happens following the receipt of a report; • the rights of complainants and survivors (e.g., to privacy, confidentiality, and protection from reprisal); and • the survivor support services available in the project area. Communication about the reporting mechanism and SEAH in general should always be carefully considered. The words and/or images used to describe the mechanism and behaviors in the code of conduct should be tested with target groups in the community for suitability and to understand whether the language used would increase or undermine trust in the reporting mechanism. For example, including images depicting violence may be triggering for survivors or may lead to the project being associated with SEAH, potentially causing an adverse reaction in the community toward women who work with the contractor. The methods for communicating with the community and with staff members should also be designed in consultation with target groups. A range of methods should be used including posters, radio, short messaging services, and community meetings. It is vital to ensure that jargon is not used, language and literacy are accounted for, and those most at risk are reached by creating and regularly disseminating information using multiple methods and communication channels.

Source: Asian Development Bank.

Receiving and responding to cases (often referred to as case handling) is a very specific set of expertise, and contractors should have their processes mapped out in their entirety via a standard operating procedure (SOP).

The forthcoming GPN on Integrating SEAH reporting and case handling into project GRMs in *ADB-Financed Projects with Civil Works* contains additional information on the appropriate handling of cases and covers MGPS 3–9 from the contractor's perspective (Table 2 and Annex B).

The contractor should have detailed procedures in place on how SEAH reports will be handled, with detailed instructions, timelines, and roles and responsibilities. The most frequent flow of events is as follows:

Receive and refer. A complaint is received. If the survivor is the complainant, they are provided with information on the available response services including health care that could prevent HIV contraction, emergency contraception, and other potentially lifesaving medical services.

- ⮕ Where possible and safe, community reporting mechanisms should link to preexisting mechanisms. Preexisting reporting mechanisms must have been tested to ensure they are appropriate.

- ⮕ SOPs should be in place to set up and handle cases (MGPS 6). This should include an information sharing protocol for interagency reporting[34] and handling of reports (for example, where a survivor reports through a shared reporting mechanism or to the police).

- ⮕ Referral protocols should be in place to inform survivors about support options available to them and the risks and benefits involved in accessing those services.

Record. A designated focal point should be appointed to receive complaints and log them in a central register.

- ⮕ The designated focal point should conduct an immediate risk assessment covering risks to the complainant and/or survivor, to the subject of concern, to other individuals, to the contractor, to the project, and to the integrity of any future investigation. Risks should have a mitigation plan that should be put in place immediately. Template for Assessment of Potential Risks Associated with Case Handling is in Annex M.

Respond. A need-to-know group is formed (usually based on the reporting lines while being cognizant of any conflict of interest). This group decides whether the report should be investigated, or whether initial information gathering is necessary before a decision is taken. If a report requires investigation, proper investigation procedures are to be followed. The survivor is provided with updates, and formal communication on the actions to be taken is sent via e-mail or letter. This should contain concrete timelines for the investigation to take place.

---

[34] Interagency reporting means the survivors or complainants can report through multiple entry points. For example, an information sharing protocol can be set up between NGOs, health care professionals, and the project. If a survivor reports to the health care service first, the health care service provider may disclose information to the project (with the survivor's permission). The forthcoming GPN on Integrating SEAH reporting and case handling into project GRMs in *ADB-Financed Projects with Civil Works* will discuss this in more depth.

SOPs should identify the different types of complaints handled and the different roles and responsibilities of handling complaints. They should contain a flow diagram outlining focal points for case handling, thresholds for reporting to others internally, guidelines on managing and maintaining confidentiality, and timelines and templates for handling cases (such as investigation TOR and risk assessments).

Based on the results of the investigation, the contractor employer of a subject of concern will take the relevant disciplinary action in accordance with the employment contract, the code of conduct, and local legislation;[35] and will inform the executing agency and/or implementing agency on the outcome regarding the subject of concern.

c. Decide Who Will Set Up and Run Reporting Mechanisms and Case Handling

The decision as to which entity or entities will implement all or some aspects of the SEAH reporting and case handling process will take place after the executing agency or implementing agency has conducted due diligence with the contractor concerning the MGPS, of which priority standards 4–9 cover SEAH reporting and case handling.

Where the contractors are unable to deliver MGPS 4–9, it is advisable to hire one or more third-party GBV/SEAH specialist service providers through the contractors or directly by executing agency or implementing agency to implement all or some elements of MGPS 4–9.

For high- and substantial-risk projects, all aspects relating to SEAH concern reporting and case handling are strongly advised to be outsourced to a third party regardless of the contractors' ability to meet MGPS 4–9.

In summary, a choice should be made as to whether (i) the contractor can deliver all aspects of SEAH reporting and case handling; or (ii) all, or components of, SEAH reporting and case handling are to be outsourced to one or more service providers. Examples of outsourcing include (i) outsourcing to an existing government actor, such as a GBV response center, to receive SEAH concerns, act as a reporting point, and/or promote reporting mechanisms in the community; (ii) outsourcing to an SEAH investigations specialist to be placed on retainer to conduct investigations; (iii) outsourcing monitoring to a third-party contractor with expertise in conducting research and monitoring on SEAH; and (iv) outsourcing the handling of workplace reporting and case handling to an organization with SEAH expertise. Third-party service providers should be selected by the executing agency and/or implementing agency in consultation with the contractor and ADB. In contexts where government GBV service providers do not have the capacity or expertise to respond to SEAH cases,[36] the third party is most likely to be an NGO operating in the project area.

---

[35] Depending on severity of the offense, the disciplinary actions may include informal warning, formal warning, mandatory additional training, loss of up to 1 week's salary, suspension of employment, termination of employment contract, and/or referral to the police or other authorities as warranted.

[36] World Bank. 2020. *Interim Technical Note: Grievance Mechanisms for Sexual Exploitation and Abuse & Sexual Harassment in World Bank-Financed Projects*. Washington, DC.

Figure 4: Flow of Decision-Making Regarding the Potential Outsourcing of Sexual Exploitation, Abuse, and Harassment Reporting and Case Handling

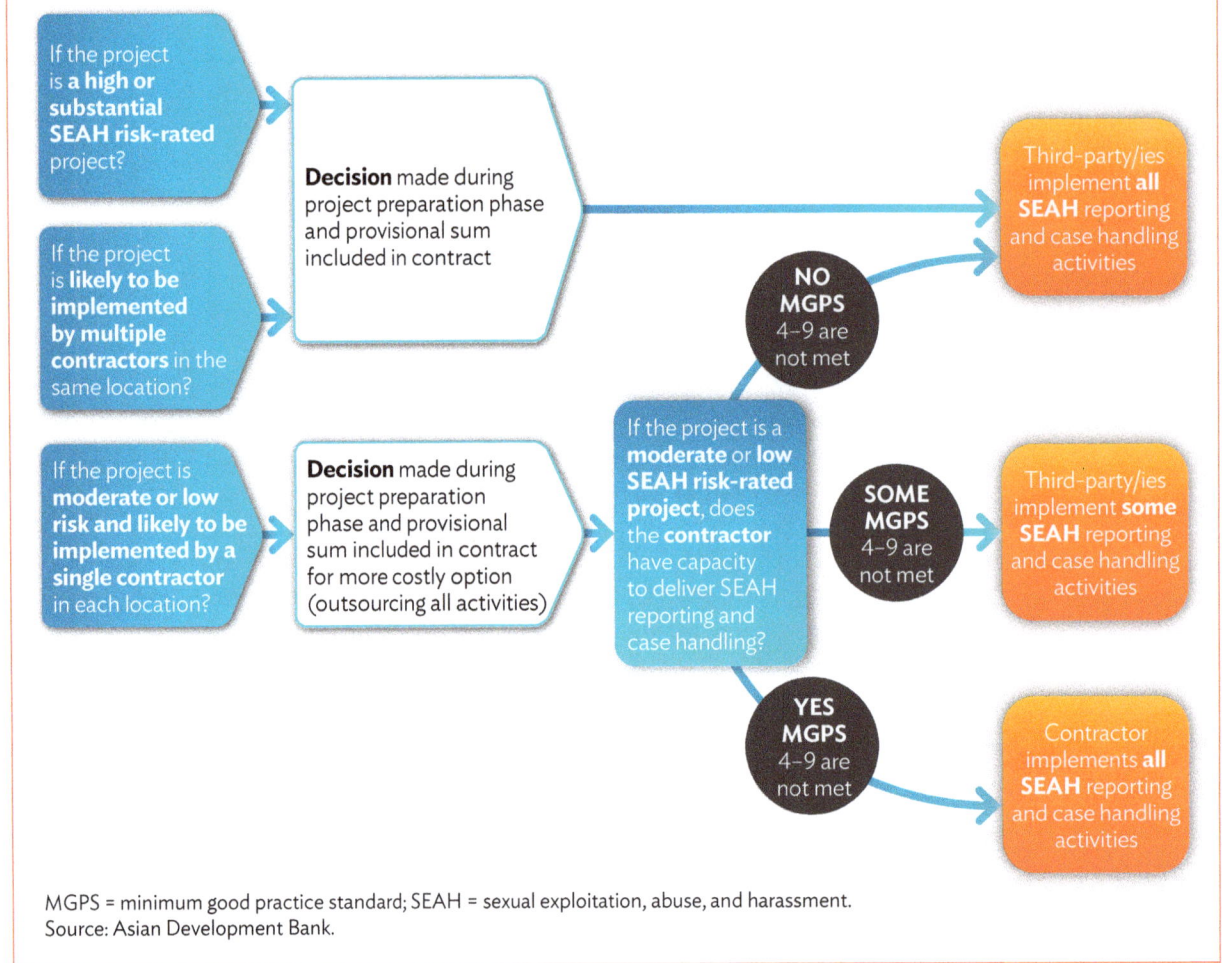

MGPS = minimum good practice standard; SEAH = sexual exploitation, abuse, and harassment.
Source: Asian Development Bank.

d. Report Upward

Contractors must report through the project implementation unit or project management office to the executing and/or implementing agency within 24 hours of receiving a report. The executing and/or implementing agency should inform the ADB project team within 24 hours of receiving the report from the contractor (Figure 5).

e. Monitor Implementation and Effectiveness of Adherence to Minimum Good Practice Standards

Adherence to the MGPS will require consistent review and reflection across all standards. However, particular emphasis should be placed on area C—reporting, handling complaints, and whistleblowing (Table 2). Case handling and monitoring work should inform learning and improvement across the MGPS and project adaptations where necessary.[37]

---

[37] For example, where a case reveals that a person was hired without appropriate vetting taking place, vetting practices should be reviewed and strengthened.

Figure 5: Reporting Flow for Reports Concerning Contractor's Staff

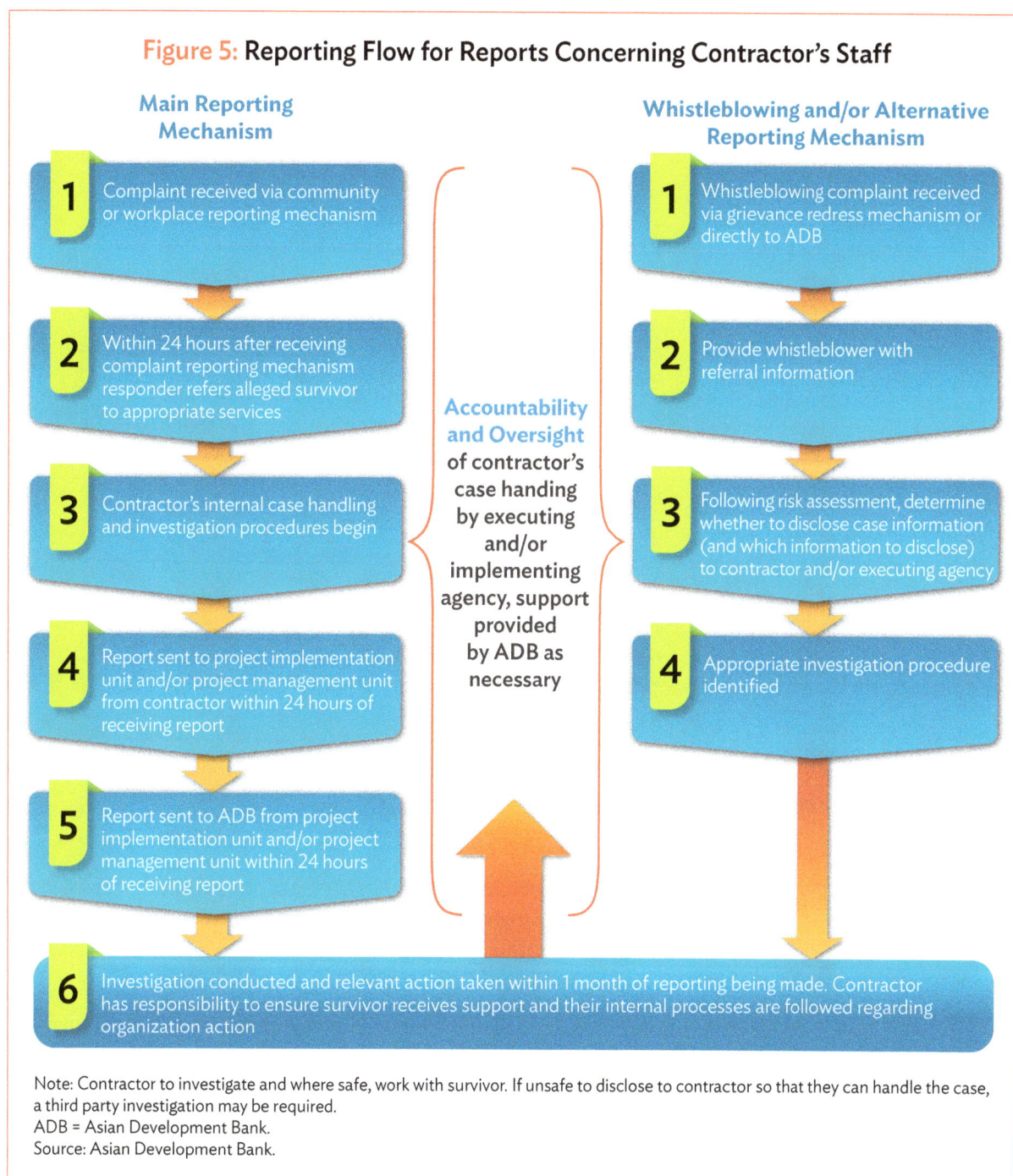

Main Reporting Mechanism

Whistleblowing and/or Alternative Reporting Mechanism

Main Reporting Mechanism

1. Complaint received via community or workplace reporting mechanism
2. Within 24 hours after receiving complaint reporting mechanism responder refers alleged survivor to appropriate services
3. Contractor's internal case handling and investigation procedures begin
4. Report sent to project implementation unit and/or project management unit from contractor within 24 hours of receiving report
5. Report sent to ADB from project implementation unit and/or project management unit within 24 hours of receiving report

Accountability and Oversight of contractor's case handing by executing and/or implementing agency, support provided by ADB as necessary

Whistleblowing and/or Alternative Reporting Mechanism

1. Whistleblowing complaint received via grievance redress mechanism or directly to ADB
2. Provide whistleblower with referral information
3. Following risk assessment, determine whether to disclose case information (and which information to disclose) to contractor and/or executing agency
4. Appropriate investigation procedure identified

6. Investigation conducted and relevant action taken within 1 month of reporting being made. Contractor has responsibility to ensure survivor receives support and their internal processes are followed regarding organization action

Note: Contractor to investigate and where safe, work with survivor. If unsafe to disclose to contractor so that they can handle the case, a third party investigation may be required.
ADB = Asian Development Bank.
Source: Asian Development Bank.

The entity operating the reporting mechanism should monitor it consistently for its performance and adherence to the guiding principles of case handling (Box 8). This should include submitting and evaluating test cases; working with the community (women, girls, and other at-risk groups) to receive their feedback; and assessing the reliability of the reporting mechanisms and handling of cases. The monitoring of the reporting mechanism and lessons learned from case handling should inform responsive adjustments to improve the relevance, safety, and effectiveness of the reporting mechanism. Annex L contains a template tool that can be used to monitor projects' approaches to addressing SEAH.

BOX 8

Core Standards for Sexual Exploitation, Abuse, and Harassment-Reporting Mechanisms in Project Grievance Redress Mechanisms

The following core standards are to be applied to the project's grievance redress mechanism and the handling of reports of sexual exploitation, abuse, and harassment (SEAH).

Confidentiality. It is important to maintain confidentiality at all stages of the process when dealing with SEAH concerns. Confidentiality is critical to satisfactory outcomes and the protection of privacy and safety of all concerned. Information relating to the concern and subsequent case handling of that concern should be shared on a need-to-know basis only and should be kept secure at all times. Breach of confidentiality for anything other than proper case management, handling, legal obligation, or whistleblowing purposes where an individual feels that the case has not been handled appropriately, is unacceptable.

Disclosure will be permitted when (i) specific permission is given by the complainant; (ii) it is required by law; (iii) it is needed to obtain specialist help for the complainant or survivor or advice on the evidence (with the permission of the complainant or where the complainant is a child, and it is in their best interest); or (iv) granted by a whistleblower regarding case handling.[a]

If breach of confidentiality is reported, it should be treated as a disciplinary matter (following appropriate investigation and/or disciplinary guidance). Breach of confidentiality may be accidental or intentional. Accidental disclosure occurs when key details about the complaint are inadvertently revealed, generally in casual conversation or when documents fall into the wrong hands. To minimize the risks of accidental disclosure, there should be clear guidelines on who is to be informed about cases and when. Intentional disclosure is more difficult to prevent. To mitigate against intentional disclosure, contractors and executing and implementing agencies need to ensure that information is limited to the "need-to-know" group, and they must remain alert to any conflict of interest and take disciplinary action against anyone who knowingly broadcasts confidential information about the case.

Responsiveness. Each complaint is responded to immediately, within a maximum of 24 hours. At a minimum, information should be provided to the survivor regarding available services, and safety should be provided to anyone connected to the incident who has requested it.

Nonretaliation. It is the right of all stakeholders to complain. Any attempt at retaliation against a complainant is considered gross misconduct and the Asian Development Bank will support the executing and/or implementing agency in taking immediate action against such behavior, including disciplinary action where appropriate.

Objectivity. Every complaint is addressed in an impartial, equitable, and objective manner.

Safety and welfare. The safety of the complainant, alleged survivor, witnesses, person or subject of complaint, and staff member is paramount. A risk assessment must be carried out for each complaint, and safety and welfare precautions must be considered before proceeding to deal with a complaint. Annex M contains a template for assessment of potential risks associated with case handling.

Survivor-centered approach. A survivor-centered approach seeks to empower the survivor by prioritizing their rights, needs, and wishes. It means ensuring that survivors have access to appropriate, accessible, and good quality services, including health care, mental health and psychological support, and legal and security support.[b] Where a survivor reports SEAH, the immediate priorities of the agency receiving the complaint should be to provide the survivor with information regarding available services and the pros and cons of accessing those services, and to offer to facilitate access to them (with a particular emphasis on health care for sexual assault survivors). A risk assessment (Annex M) should be conducted with the survivor and the subject of concern as soon as possible following the report of the incident. However, where a survivor indicates during initial disclosure that they or anyone else is at risk, their safety should be assured by working with and referring to local protection actors and a safety plan should be put in place as a matter of urgency.

continued on next page

BOX 8 *continued*

Survivors' decisions should be at the center of all actions. If the survivor is an adult, that person should decide whether they will seek referral to response services, and whether police are to be notified.[c]

Responders must understand their legal obligations, the legal limits of confidentiality, and their professional codes of practice, particularly when reporting SEAH cases to the police. The World Health Organization does not recommend mandatory reporting of gender-based violence to the police, but if a country's legislation requires mandatory reporting, the responder should inform the executing and/or implementing agencies and the potential survivor of this obligation and of any other limits to confidentiality.

Further, to make an informed decision, each individual should be provided with information on the quality of the services available, based on risk–benefit assessments of seeking support from service providers. Some of the benefits of accessing health care are to receive a compassionate response from a trained health care provider; to prevent HIV infection (within 72 hours of the incident taking place), pregnancy (within 120 hours), and/or sexually transmitted infections; to treat cuts and bruises; and to receive ongoing mental health and psychological support. No monetary compensation should be given directly to the survivor. All support services, including transportation, housing, and support requirements such as obtaining official documentation or collecting forensic evidence, can be paid only through the service provider.

Following disclosure, survivors should not be forced to attend any service. Women and men can choose whether to seek services through referrals. Survivors who are girls, boys, or adults-at-risk should participate in the referral decision (and this should be weighted in accordance with their age and their cognitive capacity), and a referral should be in the best interest of the child or adult-at-risk.[d]

[a] Only one condition needs to be in place.
[b] J. Ward. 2010. *Caring for Survivors Training Manual*. United Nations Children's Fund (UNICEF).
[c] For further information on the nuances of working with child survivors, please see ADB. Forthcoming. *Good Practice Note on Integrating SEAH Reporting and Case Handling into Project Grievance Redress Mechanisms in ADB-Financed Projects with Civil Works*. Manila.
[d] For more information, see Interagency Standing Committee. 2015. *How to Support Survivors of Gender-Based Violence When a GBV Actor Is Not Available in Your Area: A Step-By-Step Pocket Guide for Humanitarian Practitioners*.
Source: Based on K. Samara-Wickrama, C. Heemskerk, R. Ivory, and L. Heaven-Taylor. 2015. *Guidelines for Investigations: A guide for Humanitarian Organisations on Receiving and Investigating Allegations of Abuse, Exploitation, Fraud or Corruption by Their Own Staff* (second edition). CHS Alliance.

f. Complete Due Diligence According to the Minimum Good Practice Standards with Their Subcontractors

Contractors are responsible for ensuring that subcontractors and suppliers meet the MGPS and for supporting them in the design of their own SEAH action plans where these are necessary.

g. Provide Regular Updates to Executing and/or Implementing Agencies

In all quarterly and annual project reports, the contractor should make a declaration that affirms that all allegations of SEAH have been reported and handled in accordance with their policies, practices, and procedures for case handling, which should adhere to the MGPS. Where there are delays in reporting without justification, the executing and/or implementing agency may take action to address this in accordance with contract provisions.

Where case handling identifies areas within SEAH prevention, mitigation, and response that need strengthening, the executing and/or implementing agency can support the contractor to address the gaps.

The contractor will be expected to identify lessons learned from each case reported and improve their prevention, mitigation, and response to SEAH accordingly within six months of case closure.

2. Detailed Executing and Implementing Agency Actions

a. Set Up Reporting Mechanisms for Receiving Sexual Exploitation, Abuse, and Harassment Cases from Contractors

As noted elsewhere in this publication, all incidents of SEAH reported to contractors should be reported to the executing and implementing agencies via the project implementation unit or project management office within 24 hours of the contractor receiving the report. The executing and/or implementing agency should inform ADB about all reported incidents of SEAH within 24 hours of receiving them from the contractor.

Annex N contains an example of a recommended reporting form template for executing and implementing agencies to report to ADB. The executing agencies, implementing agencies, and contractors may wish to adapt this reporting form.

The contractor's reporting mechanism should be the primary means of reporting for staff and community members affected by project-related SEAH. However, complainants may choose to use the reporting mechanism of the executing and/or implementing agency. They may also opt to report directly to the relevant ADB operations department or resident mission if they feel that their case has not been satisfactorily handled. Or if, after failed efforts with the contractor or executing or implementing agency, complainants feel that reporting directly to ADB is for the public good (such as where large numbers of SEAH incidents are occurring in a project with no or ineffective action).[38] It would be prudent for executing and/or implementing agencies to hire an SEAH expert to handle these types of reports if there is a lack of internal capacity to do so.

Alternative reporting routes should be included in the promotional materials, communication plan, and training courses for staff members.

b. Ensure Staff Members Are Appropriately Able to Handle Cases, Oversee Case Handling by Contractors, and Seek Accountability of Contractors on Cases Handled

To provide oversight and accountability on case handling by contractors, it is important that the executing and/or implementing agency staff tasked to oversee contractors' cases are skilled and trained in case handling, experienced in conducting investigations, and providing support. The executing and/or implementing agency should set the system of reporting and accountability, and the contractor shall be unique to each project. If the executing and/or implementing agency receives a report regarding an SEAH concern and does not receive a level of information that reassures them that the guiding principles of case handling are being followed (Box 7), they should seek reassurance from the contractor immediately. The primary focus should be to ensure that the contractor has facilitated referrals for the alleged survivor, and has conducted risk and safety assessments for the

---

[38] As this GPN applies only to new sovereign projects with civil works during the pilot period designated by ADB, the GPN, and its application to such projects during such period is not subject to ADB's Accountability Mechanism.

alleged survivor and the subject of concern. This approach provides crucial oversight, accountability, guidance, and support where contractors may need it.

c. Engage in Case Handling of Incidents Involving Their Own Staff

ADB should be informed within 24 hours regarding reports of SEAH incidents received by the executing and/or implementing agency where the subject of concern is a member of their own staff whose position is paid for with ADB funds, and where the alleged survivor is a member of the staff engaged by the project contractor or a member of a project-affected community. In handling cases involving their own staff, executing and/or implementing agencies may be guided by the *GPN on Integrating SEAH Reporting and Case Handling into Project GRMs in ADB-Financed Projects with Civil Works*.

d. Deliver Executing and/or Implementing Agency Action Plan Targets for Establishing Organizational Systems and Protocols for Sexual Exploitation, Abuse, and Harassment Prevention, Mitigation, and Response

Within the first year of the project, the executing and/or implementing agency should complete their action plan activities related to setting up institutional systems and protocols for SEAH prevention, mitigation, and response.[39] With the organizational systems and protocols in place, the rest of the planned actions for monitoring and safeguarding can continue throughout the lifetime of the project.

Contractor selection will be accompanied by a due diligence process designed to ensure all contractors meet the MGPS. Actions under MGPS sections A, B, C, E, and H should be prioritized, and for projects rated substantial- and high-risk, implementation should be delayed until these priority standards can be met. Contractors' SEAH action plans are best implemented in a phased manner. Establishment of the SEAH prevention, mitigation, and response systems and protocols should not go on for longer than a year. Contractors' SEAH action plans should put in place a road map for filling gaps in contractor's policies, practices, and procedures. However, efforts on SEAH prevention, mitigation, and response should continue for the duration of the project in accordance with the MGPS; and executing and implementing agencies must continue to monitor contractors' SEAH prevention, mitigation, and response efforts.

If the contractor is unable to handle cases or effectively respond to SEAH, a third-party SEAH specialist or service provider can be hired to deliver MGPS 4–9.

e. Implement Plans to Ensure Response Services Are in Place and Appropriate

During project preparation, executing and/or implementing agency are responsible for mapping SEAH services and planning ways to fill gaps in service provision. The expectations to fill gaps vary according to the risk level of the project. Response services should be put in place or strengthened during the inception phase of the project. No project implementation involving interaction with project-affected communities should occur before the appropriate level of services has been put

---

[39]   When new contractors come in, they should develop their own SEAH action plans. They will have up to one year from their contract start date to complete the actions. This period can be shortened on a case-by-case basis to ensure that the systems and protocols are in place.

in place. However, further consultation with the community may continue beyond the project inception phase if the executing or implementing agency has assessed the associated risks.

f. Conduct Monitoring for Each Contractor

The executing or implementing agency should conduct field visits to monitor contractor performance on SEAH prevention, mitigation, and response at least twice a year for substantial- and high-risk projects. Monitoring should focus on assessing their practical application of the MGPS. Monitoring guidance is in Annex L.

g. Respond to Inadequate Handling of Sexual Exploitation, Abuse, and Harassment Concerns by Contractors

Where SEAH risks or allegations arise in an ADB-financed pilot project, the executing agency, implementing agency, and contractors will develop measures to mitigate risk and facilitate resolution. Should the issue persist or should the executing or implementing agency assess that contractors are not addressing the issue adequately despite dialogue and support, the executing or implementing agencies will decide on appropriate actions including possible suspension or termination of contract.

3.   Detailed ADB Actions

a. Monitor Implementation of Sexual Exploitation, Abuse, and Harassment Action Plan

The executing or implementing agencies will regularly update ADB on progress toward completing actions in their SEAH action plan. Project reporting will include a section on completed SEAH prevention, mitigation, and response actions. The monitoring of SEAH as part of the project review missions can further supplement the SEAH action plan process.

b. Oversee Case Handling

An SEAH concern reported to a project using the contractor's reporting mechanism should be reported to the executing and/or implementing agencies within 24 hours of the complaint being made. The executing and/or implementing agencies should inform ADB within 24 hours of receiving it from the contractor. Where a complaint is made directly to the executing and/or implementing agencies, it should similarly be reported to ADB within 24 hours of receipt of the complaint. Reports should be sent to the designated e-mail address copying the project officer in the ADB operations department. Templates for case reporting are in Annex N.

The following questions should be considered during the monitoring process:

- ⮑ How many and what type of SEAH allegations have been made during the reporting period? This may vary depending on the duration of the reporting period, the risk categorization of the project, the country context, and the sector or work.

- Have cases been resolved? The principle of zero tolerance to inaction on SEAH should be always followed. There is an expectation that each allegation will be reviewed, and an investigation will be launched if deemed necessary. Any discrepancies between the number of allegations and the number of cases where complaints are upheld should be duly noted. A large discrepancy may indicate that investigations are not being handled appropriately.

- Have survivors been offered or received relevant support, including medical, legal, safety, and psychosocial support? It is important to note that not all survivors may want to access support services, so there may be a discrepancy between the number of survivors and the number of survivors that have accessed support services. However, all survivors should be offered support unconditionally.

It is recommended to use a proportionate approach when reviewing allegations, prioritizing cases where the risk to survivors is most severe and where investigations and survivor support are likely to be problematic.

The following actions are recommended and in line with the principles of this GPN:

- Request information on the welfare of survivors and whether survivors have been offered relevant quality support and/or referrals by the contractors.

- When necessary, support the executing and/or implementing agency in identifying whether a third party may be better placed to investigate. It is important to note that ADB does not conduct investigations on behalf of executing agencies, implementing agencies, contractors, or subcontractors.

- Review risk assessments to check whether appropriate risk mitigations have been delivered to ensure the safety of the survivor and other parties.

- Review investigation reports for high priority and whistleblowing cases.

ANNEXES

Sexual Exploitation, Abuse, and Harassment Key Concepts

This good practice note (GPN) uses the following definitions of sexual exploitation, abuse, and harassment (SEAH). They align with those of the multilateral development banks and other key development actors.

Gender-based violence	An umbrella term for any harmful act that is perpetrated against a person's will, and that is based on socially constructed and ascribed differences in power between men and women. Although violence may be based on a number of inequalities, the inequality between men and women in society is the focus of the definition of gender-based violence (GBV). Inequalities based on power fluctuate over time and location. Frequently perpetrated types of GBV and the acceptability of GBV shift from context to context. GBV is a continuum and includes acts that inflict physical, sexual, or mental harm or suffering; threats of such acts; coercion; harassment; psychological abuse; and other deprivations of liberty. These acts can occur in public or in private. The term GBV is most commonly used to underscore how systemic inequality between men and women, which exists in every society in the world, acts as a unifying and foundational characteristic of most forms of violence perpetrated against women and girls.

It is important to acknowledge that men, women, boys, girls, and nonbinary individuals can experience violence, but GBV research, policymaking, and programming has largely focused on women and girls because structural and systemic gender inequality privileges men with greater power and resources, rendering women and girls at greater risk of violence being perpetrated against them. As a result, GBV is often used interchangeably with the term violence against women and girls (VAWG). VAWG is sharply focused on women and girls as survivors of violence, whereas GBV could include violence against men, boys, and nonbinary individuals, provided the violence stems from the perceived rejection of socially ascribed gender norms of masculinity. |
Sexual exploitation, abuse, and harassment	SEAH is the term used to refer to sexual exploitation, abuse, and harassment. Although sexual exploitation, abuse, and harassment can occur anywhere in society, when used as an umbrella term within the official development assistance (ODA) sector the term refers to acts of SEAH perpetrated by those working in, with, or through ODA actors and their projects. This includes within a program setting, as a part of work travel, or in online interactions. Service users, members of the community, and staff working in the ODA sector are vulnerable to being targeted for SEAH.[1]
Sexual exploitation	Sexual exploitation means "any actual or attempted abuse of a position of vulnerability, differential power, or trust for sexual purposes, including but not limited to profiting monetarily, socially, or politically from the sexual abuse of another."[2]
Sexual abuse	Sexual abuse means the "actual or threatened physical intrusion of a sexual nature, whether by force or unequal or coercive conditions" (footnote 2).

[1] Resource and Support Hub. 2021. *Understanding SEAH and GBV*. UK Aid: London.
[2] Task Team on the SEA [Sexual Exploitation and Abuse] Glossary for the Special Coordinator on improving the United Nations response to sexual exploitation and abuse. 2017. *Glossary on Sexual Exploitation and Abuse*. Second Edition.

continued on next page

Definitions, *continued*

Sexual harassment	Sexual harassment at work is "any unwelcome conduct of a sexual nature that might reasonably be expected or be perceived to cause offense or humiliation, when such conduct interferes with work; is made a condition of employment; or creates an intimidating, hostile, or offensive work environment."[3] However, sexual harassment can occur outside the workplace and outside working hours, including during official travel, social functions related to work, and/or online. Sexual harassment at work may also include the disclosure, or discussion of, an individual's sexual orientation or gender identity without an individual's express permission. Sexual harassment can take the form of an isolated incident or repeated incidents. Sexual harassment does not need to be between colleagues and can occur within society in general. It can involve teasing, offhand comment, or sexualized jokes or gestures and may involve any conduct of a verbal, nonverbal, or physical nature
Survivor-centered approach	A survivor-centered approach is based on the principles of privacy, confidentiality, agency, dignity, respect, and nondiscrimination. A survivor-centered approach guides professionals—regardless of their role—in their engagement with survivors who have experienced sexual or other forms of violence. The survivor-centered approach aims to create a supportive environment in which the survivor's interests are respected and prioritized, and in which the survivor is treated with dignity and respect. The approach helps to promote the survivor's recovery and ability to identify and express needs and wishes, and to reinforce the survivor's capacity to make decisions about possible interventions.[4]
Prevention of sexual exploitation, abuse, and harassment	Prevention of SEAH refers to taking action to stop SEAH from first occurring (e.g., by scaling up activities that promote gender equality or address practices that contribute to SEAH).[5] This could be through supporting gender equality-focused programming, social norms, or behavior change communication work.
Mitigation of sexual exploitation, abuse, and harassment	Mitigation of SEAH refers to reducing the risk of exposure to SEAH. This may be through increased lighting on an infrastructure project, or ensuring that well-lit, lockable latrines are put in place on project sites. Mitigation work centers around working with women and girls and other at-risk populations in project design and mapping SEAH issues with them, regularly identifying SEAH hotspots, and seeking to mitigate the risk of SEAH in those locations through project activities. Mitigation work seeks to reduce the risk of SEAH occurring or of being exacerbated by project activities or actions.
Sexual exploitation, abuse, and harassment response	Responding to allegations, issues, and concerns regarding SEAH in a comprehensive manner including setting up and promoting accessible reporting mechanisms that are regularly tested and monitored, being able to refer a survivor to appropriate and safe services, and undertaking timely and transparent investigations into allegations.

[3] United Nations (UN) Secretariat. 2019. *Addressing Discrimination, Harassment, Including Sexual Harassment, and Abuse of Authority*. *Secretary-General's bulletin ST/SGB/2019/8*. New York.

[4] World Bank. 2018. *Good Practice Note Addressing Gender-Based Violence In Investment Project Financing Involving Major Civil Works*. Washington, DC.

[5] Inter-Agency Standing Committee. 2015. *Guidelines for Integrating Gender-Based Violence Interventions in Humanitarian Action: Reducing Risk, Promoting Resilience and Aiding Recovery*.

Children can be and have been particularly affected by SEAH, and this can cause significant long-term consequences for affected individuals. This GPN uses the following additional definitions, specifically in relation to children and SEAH:

Child	A person under the age of 18 unless under the law applicable to the child, majority is attained earlier.[6]
Child sexual abuse	When a child is forced or persuaded to take part in sexual activities. This may involve physical contact or noncontact activities.[7]
Child sexual exploitation	"Is a form of child sexual abuse. It occurs where an individual or group takes advantage of an imbalance of power to coerce, manipulate or deceive a child or young person under the age of 18 into sexual activity: (a) in exchange for something the survivor needs or wants; and/or (b) for the financial advantage or increased status of the perpetrator or person who persuades/facilitates the exploitation. The survivor of child sexual exploitation is to be considered a survivor even if the sexual activity appears consensual (as sexual contact with a child is never consensual). Child sexual exploitation does not always involve physical contact; it can also occur through the use of technology" (footnote 7).

Other useful definitions are as follows:

Adult at risk	Any person who is aged 18 years or over and is at risk of abuse or neglect because of their needs for care and support. This can include mental health issues, learning or physical disability, sensory impairment, age or illness, and inability to take care of themselves or to protect themselves against significant harm or exploitation.
Complainant	The person who files a complaint regarding wrongdoing. This can be the alleged survivor, a witness, or another person who becomes aware of the wrongdoing, or a whistleblower (see definition below).
Disclosure	Disclosure is the process of revealing information. Disclosure about abuse can be communicated directly or indirectly. The term disclosure is preferred over identification as it indicates that the individual sharing details of an incident or concern has decided to discuss the incident with the organization. An individual who discloses abuse may become a complainant.
Discrimination	Discrimination refers to treating a person or a group of people less favorably than another person or group based on protected characteristics.[8] For the purposes of this GPN, protected characteristics include age, disability, gender identity, marriage and civil partnerships, pregnancy and maternity, ethnic identity, race, religion or belief, sex, sexual orientation, perceived or actual class status, education background, trades union membership or affiliation, political beliefs, and nationality. This is an inexhaustive list. Discrimination may manifest in different ways in different locations and protected characteristics may need to be evaluated differently. For example, in South Asia, the definition may be broadened to incorporate discrimination based on caste.
Informed consent	Consent is when a person makes an informed choice to agree freely and voluntarily to do something. There is no consent when agreement is obtained through • the use of threats, force, or other forms of coercion, abduction, fraud, manipulation, deception, or misrepresentation; • the use of a threat to withhold a benefit to which the person is already entitled; or • a promise made to the person to provide a benefit.[9]

[6] United Nations Children's Fund (UNICEF) UK. 2021. *UN Convention on the Rights the Child, Article 1.*

[7] UNICEF. Forthcoming. *Review of National Educational Strategies to Prevent Child Sexual Abuse and Exploitation in East Asia and the Pacific.* Bangkok: UNICEF.

[8] Government of the United Kingdom. 2010. *Equality Act 2010.* London.

[9] Office for the Coordination of Humanitarian Affairs (OCHA), United Nations Commissioner for Human Rights, and International Rescue Committee. 2006. *The GBV IMS, GBV Classification Tool.*

continued on next page

Gender	The socially constructed roles, attributes, opportunities, and relationships that a given society considers appropriate for men and women. These expectations differ from society to society and change over time. In many societies, it has been recognized that there are more than two genders. However, "men/boys" and "women/girls" are the most commonly recognized genders and are, therefore, used throughout this guidance.[10]
Gender expression	Gender expression is each person's presentation of their gender through physical appearance—including dress, hairstyles, accessories, and cosmetics—and mannerisms, speech, behavioral patterns, names, and personal references. Gender expression may or may not conform to a person's gender identity.[11]
Gender identity	Gender identity is understood to refer to each person's deeply felt internal and individual experience of gender, which may or may not correspond with the sex assigned at birth, including the personal sense of the body (which may involve, if freely chosen, modification of bodily appearance or function by medical, surgical, or other means) and other expressions of gender, including dress, speech, and mannerisms (footnote 11).
Nonbinary or third gender	Nonbinary and third gender are terms used to describe people whose gender identity falls outside the male–female binary. They can also describe persons who identify as both male and female (bi-gender), do not identify with any gender (agender), or identify as a mix of different genders (e.g., male, female, and agender on different days) (footnote 11).
Sex	Sex refers to the biological differences that act as a marker upon which male or female sex is assigned at birth (footnote 11).
Sex characteristics	Sex characteristics are each person's physical features relating to sex, including genitalia and other sexual and reproductive anatomy, chromosomes, hormones, and secondary physical features emerging from puberty (footnote 11).
Sexual orientation	Sexual orientation is understood to refer to each person's capacity for profound emotional, affectional, and sexual attraction to, and intimate and sexual relations with, individuals of a different gender or the same gender or more than one gender (footnote 11).
SOGIESC	SOGIESC is an acronym for sexual orientation, gender identity and expression, and sexual characteristics. Beyond sex and gender, the SOGIESC perspective offers a multidimensional perspective as an alternative view in understanding nonconforming or atypical genders.[12] "People with diverse SOGIESC" is an umbrella term for all people whose sexual orientations, gender identities, gender expressions, and/or sex characteristics place them outside culturally mainstream categories.[13]
Subject of concern	The individual or group of individuals who have been accused of wrongdoing and breaches code of conduct—but there is not yet evidence that this claim is true. When the claim has been proven, this GPN uses the word "perpetrator" or "perpetrators."
Survivor	This GPN uses the term "survivor" to describe the person who has experienced SEAH. While the term "survivor" may be used interchangeably with "victim," the use of "survivor" is more empowering and implies resiliency.
Transgender	An umbrella term used to describe a wide range of identities whose appearance and characteristics are perceived as gender atypical, including transsexual people, cross-dressers (sometimes referred to as transvestites), and people who identify as third gender.[14]
Whistleblower	A whistleblower is any person or persons who, in good faith and voluntarily, reports, or is believed to be about to report, or is believed to have reported suspected misconduct. The term "whistleblowing" is a specific form of reporting and should not be confused with broader reporting within organizations or within the community. Whistleblowers often have protection within legal frameworks.

[10] S. Neville, T. Salam, V. Naidu, and E. Fraser. 2020. *Addressing Gender-Based Violence and Harassment, Emerging Good Practice for the Private Sector*. European Bank for Reconstruction and Development, CDC Group, and International Finance Corporation.

[11] C. Thomas and C. Weber. 2019. *Information paper on protection against sexual orientation, gender identity and expression and sexual characteristics (SOGIESC) discrimination*. Geneva: International Labour Organization.

[12] UN Human Rights Council. 2011. *UN Human Rights Council 17/19 on Sexual Orientation and Gender Identity*.

[13] International Organization for Migration. 2020. *SOGIESC Full Glossary of Terms*.

[14] UN Human Rights Office. Free & Equal. *Definitions*.

Minimum Good Practice Standards on Addressing Sexual Exploitation, Abuse, and Harassment

Executing and implementing agencies should be able to ensure that contractors have the following in place as a minimum.

Area	Minimum Good Practice Standards
A. SEAH policy (Priority standard)	1. Have a policy or a combination of relevant policies that address SEAH in the workplace and in the community.
B. Code of conduct (Priority standard)	2. Have a clear employee code of conduct that prohibits all forms of SEAH and requires regular training requirements for all personnel.
C. Reporting, handling of complaints, and whistleblowing (standards 4–9 may be outsourced to an appropriate specialized partner) (Priority standards)	3. Have, or be willing to develop, a comprehensive and confidential SEAH reporting mechanism for escalating and managing concerns and complaints. This should include the option of anonymous reporting and whistleblowing. They must be accessible to workers and community members who come into contact with contractors' staff and workers.
	4. Be able to work with communities and constituencies to analyze the most appropriate and accessible means to report concerns and complaints. Multiple methods to do so must be put in place.
	5. Be able to promote the code of conduct and reporting mechanisms to the staff and the community or communities in the project area.
	6. Have a clear internal handling framework (standard operating procedure) to respond appropriately to all concerns and support the survivor in a survivor-centered way.
	7. Have identified and risk-assessed services available within the project context to ensure safe referrals of survivors can take place.
	8. Have in-house trained investigators or have identified an appropriate external investigation resource.
	9. Have a whistleblowing policy that includes SEAH.
D. Human resources	10. Ensure all staff, contractors, volunteers, and other representatives have at least a mandatory induction training when they commence employment and annual refresher training on the code of conduct and the organization's SEAH policy and whistleblowing policy, or a combination of relevant policies.
	11. Have a recruitment approach that includes specific interview question(s) that draw out applicants' attitudes and values in relation to at-risk groups.
E. Risk management (Priority standards)	12. Have a comprehensive and effective risk management framework in place that includes reference to SEAH and the creation of a central register of SEAH reports.
	13. Have requirements for maintaining and updating the central register of SEAH concerns, including information confidentiality requirements.
F. Working with subcontractors and suppliers	14. Include information on SEAH risks and expectations in contracts.
	15. Review subcontractors' policies against these minimum standards or similar standards. Where subcontractors do not have policies, practices, and procedures in place, subcontractors and suppliers should adhere to the contracting agency's code of conduct.
	16. Provide information to subcontractors and suppliers about project reporting mechanisms and the need to ensure these are in place.

continued on next page

continued from previous page

Area	Minimum Good Practice Standards
G. Workplace design	17. Include SEAH in regular workplace safety assessments, including working accommodation, transportation, and site safety.
H. Leadership and accountability (Priority standards)	18. Communicate regularly regarding their zero tolerance to inaction on SEAH utilizing internal and external communication routes.
	19. Have clear guidelines for monitoring and overseeing implementation of the policy or policies.
	20. Have the capacity to be able to report allegations within 24 hours to the executing and implementing agencies.

SEAH = sexual exploitation, abuse, and harassment.
Source: Asian Development Bank.

Summary Table of Actions to Address Sexual Exploitation, Abuse, and Harassment in the Projects Cycle with Civil Works

The table summarizes actions required by responsible stakeholders to ensure sexual exploitation, abuse, and harassment is considered and addressed at different stages of the project cycle and further summarizes the roles and responsibilities of executing agencies, implementing agencies, and contractors.

When in ADB Project Cycle	Who Is Responsible?	Summary SEAH Actions	Whether Action Is Required, by SEAH Risk Level			
			Low	Moderate	Substantial	High
Project Preparation	**1. Conducting risk assessment**					
	ADB	(i) Conduct initial discussions with the government: Work with the government to discuss SEAH risk, mitigations, and expectations regarding their role as executing and/or implementing agency and the role of the contractors and consultants in the prevention, mitigation, and response to SEAH within the project.	✔	✔	✔	✔
	ADB	(ii) Complete project's SEAH risk categorization.	✔	✔	✔	✔
	ADB	(iii) Include SEAH in gender mainstreaming work where applicable.	✔	✔	✔	✔
	2. Supporting executing and implementing agencies in due diligence					
	ADB, executing agency, and implementing agency	(i) Work with executing and implementing agencies to understand their skills and gaps in delivering due diligence of contractors.	✔	✔	✔	✔
	ADB	(ii) Consult with other multilateral development banks to develop a coordinated SEAH plans where there is an overlap and to understand if there are any major concerns regarding SEAH.	✔	✔	✔	✔
	Executing agency and implementing agency	(iii) Develop executing agency and implementing agency SEAH action plan with support needs and costs clearly indicated, including ensuring SEAH response services are in place and appropriate in project sites.	✔ Compliance focused[a]	✔ Compliance focused[a]	✔ Compliance and content focused[a]	✔ Compliance and content focused[a]

continued on next page

continued from previous page

When in ADB Project Cycle	Who Is Responsible?	Summary SEAH Actions	Whether Action Is Required, by SEAH Risk Level			
			Low	*Moderate*	*Substantial*	*High*
Project Preparation	**Executing agency and implementing agency**	(iv) Conduct service mapping and assess services available to respond appropriately to SEAH in project sites and cost out plans to fill gaps in service provision. Basic plans for projects rated *low* and *moderate* risk may focus on health services only. Projects rated *substantial* and *high* risk should have more comprehensive plans that cover health, protection, legal, and psychosocial services.	✔ Basic	✔ Basic	✔ Comprehensive	✔ Comprehensive
	Executing agency and implementing agency	(v) Conduct an in-depth SEAH analysis or assessment.	o	*	✔	✔
	3. Procurement[b]					
	Executing agency and implementing agency	(i) Based on the issues identified during project preparation and due diligence, include the SEAH requirements and obligations of both contracting parties in the bidding documents.	✔	✔	✔	✔
	Executing agency and implementing agency	(ii) Include in the bidding documents requirements for the cost of the SEAH action plan as appropriate.	✔	✔	✔	✔
	Executing agency and implementing agency	(iii) Include the bidding documents any planned necessary costs to fill gaps identified during service mapping.	✔	✔	✔	✔
	Executing agency and implementing agency	(iv) Include in the bidding documents the cost of addressing SEAH implementation, either built into the unit rates and or as specified provisional sum for activities whose scope and cost cannot be estimated accurately in advance.	✔	✔	✔	✔
	Executing agency and implementing agency	(v) Include SEAH MGPS in the bidding documents to be used by bidders for self-assessment and development of contractor's SEAH action plan.	✔	✔	✔	✔
	Bidders	(vi) Conduct self-assessment according to the ADB SEAH MGPS and develop a costed contractor's SEAH action plan.	✔ Compliance focused[a]	✔ Compliance focused[a]	✔ Compliance and content focused[a]	✔ Compliance and content focused[a]
	Bidders	(vii) As per requirements of bid documents, submit a declaration of whether they have had a contract terminated or suspended or a performance security called for reasons relating to past poor performance on SEAH. Demonstrate how they have improved their internal systems to be able address the past poor performance.	✔	✔	✔	✔
	Executing agency and implementing agency	(viii) Include requirement in bidding documents for contractors to report to executing and implementing agencies any SEAH incident within 24 hours upon receipt of a report or complaint.	✔	✔	✔	✔

continued on next page

continued from previous page

When in ADB Project Cycle	Who Is Responsible?	Summary SEAH Actions	Whether Action Is Required, by SEAH Risk Level			
			Low	Moderate	Substantial	High
Project Implementation and Contract Management	**1. Contractor implementation**					
	Contractors	(i) Implement the contractor's SEAH action plan, including standard operating procedures for case handling.	✔	✔	✔	✔
	Contractors in consultation with executing agency and implementing agency	(ii) Assess whether a third-party external service provider is needed.	o	*	✔	✔
	Contractors	(iii) Set up or adapt existing reporting mechanisms within the workplace and within the project-affected community.	✔	✔	✔	✔
	Contractors	(iv) Receive, refer, record, respond, and report upward.	✔	✔	✔	✔
	Contractors	(v) Report cases to the executing agency and implementing agency within 24 hours of receiving a concern.	✔	✔	✔	✔
	Contractors	(vi) Monitor and report to executing and/implementing agency on implementation and effectiveness of adherence to the SEAH MGPS.	✔	✔	✔	✔
	Contractors	(vii) Complete SEAH due diligence with subcontractors.	✔	✔	✔	✔
	Contractors	(viii) Provide regular updates to executing agency and implementing agency.	✔	✔	✔	✔
	2. Executing agency and implementing agency implementation					
	Executing agency and implementing agency	(i) Put in place reporting mechanisms for receiving reports on SEAH cases from contractors and a clear handling framework, and communicate them to contractors.	✔	✔	✔	✔
	Executing agency and implementing agency	(ii) Ensure staff are appropriately able to handle cases, oversee case handling by contractors, and seek accountability of contractors on cases handled.	✔	✔	✔	✔
	Executing agency and implementing agency	(iii) Engage in case handling of SEAH incidents involving their own staff members.	✔	✔	✔	✔
	Executing agency and implementing agency	(iv) Ensure that all systems and mechanisms for SEAH action plan are in place by the end of the first year of project effectiveness.	✔	✔	✔	✔
	Executing agency and implementing agency	(v) Update status of project SEAH action plan implementation when preparing regular project progress reports.	✔	✔	✔	✔

continued on next page

continued from previous page

When in ADB Project Cycle	Who Is Responsible?	Summary SEAH Actions	Whether Action Is Required, by SEAH Risk Level			
			Low	Moderate	Substantial	High
	Executing agency and implementing agency	(vi) Implement plans to ensure SEAH response services are in place and appropriate.	✔	✔	✔	✔
	Executing agency and implementing agency	(vii) Conduct SEAH MGPS monitoring for each contractor twice a year.	o	*	✔	✔
	3. ADB					
	ADB	(i) Regularly monitor executing agency and implementing agency SEAH action plan implementation.	✔	✔	✔	✔
	ADB	(ii) Oversee and provide support to executing agency and implementing agency where necessary.	✔	✔	✔	✔

✔ = required; * = recommended; o = not applicable; ADB = Asian Development Bank; MGPS = minimum good practice standards; SEAH = sexual exploitation, abuse, and harassment.

a   Compliance-focused assessment checks the presence or absence of policies, practices, and procedures. Content-focused assessment investigates the quality of available services. Compliance- and content-focused assessment is explained in section E of the good practice note.

b   When bidding takes place during project implementation, the same requirements listed in the preparation stage—items 1.3 (i)–(viii)—should apply.

Source: Asian Development Bank.

ANNEX D
Sexual Exploitation, Abuse, and Harassment Risk Assessment Tool

Project Summary

Project Details

Project Name

Project Number

Department

Division

Gender Category

Country

Loan Number

Name of EA/IA

Resettlement

Environment

Indigenious

Project Status

Weighted Results

Country Context

KII results

Project Design

Project Implementation

Project Workforce

Total Score

Update Risk Indicators

Last Modified:

Last Modified by:

Active link to SEAH Risk Assessment Tool is accessible to ADB staff and consultants.

ANNEX E
Sexual Exploitation, Abuse, and Harassment Risks in ADB's Key Sectors of Operations

A.   Construction and Infrastructure Development

Construction activities in all sectors carry a *high* risk of sexual exploitation, abuse, and harassment (SEAH). There are several reasons for this, including the typically large and primarily male workforce engaged during construction. This workforce may consist of temporary workers on short contracts who either live in on-site accommodation or within the host communities. Large, male workforces increase the potential for nuanced or overt demands for the sexual services of women in the surrounding community. Further, where construction projects involve land acquisition and resettlement and/or relocation, bringing community members into direct contact with contractor and subcontractor staff who wield implicit power over their pending claims and entitlements, women and other marginalized groups are at greater risk of being targeted for SEAH. Examples of SEAH risks in such projects are as follows:

- Construction workers may sexually exploit young boys and girls from surrounding communities who play near the construction site.

- A manager of a resettlement and/or relocation process may tell a community member that they will receive higher compensation or more benefits if they engage in sex with them.

- Drivers employed by the contractor to transport construction materials to and from the site may pay community members for sex.

- Women from the community who are engaged as construction workers on the project may experience sexual harassment by male colleagues or supervisors.

- Female workers may be targeted for SEAH by male construction workers, creating a hostile working environment.

- Government enforcers or private security assisting in construction, relocation, or resettlement activities may perpetrate SEAH against members of the affected population.

B.   Agribusiness

Agriculture is characterized by a high concentration of female workers in unskilled, labor-intensive tasks with limited opportunities for skills upgrading. Projects in agricultural settings can increase the risk of SEAH because of their seasonal work, remote locations, and use of migrant and/or temporary labor.

- Companies working with tight seasonal deadlines attempt to incentivize productivity through the use of performance-related pay. Managers may use these bonus schemes and piece-rate systems as opportunities to demand sexual favors from workers.

- Female workers in remote locations who are landless or working on dispersed workplaces may experience sexual harassment by male supervisors.

- Rural female workers may be sexually abused by contractor or project staff and told to keep quiet about the incident or face losing their jobs.

C. Urban Infrastructure Development

Urban infrastructure development projects (including energy, water, and transport infrastructure) are often in settings that combine multidimensional and intersectional challenges, such as aging populations, informal settlements, densely populated areas, and climate shocks, which can increase residents' vulnerability. The heightened risks of SEAH that such settings entail include the following:

- Women who head households may be pressured into granting sexual favors in exchange for access to newly established services.

- Road workers may sexually harass girls walking to and from school near the project site.

- Female transport workers may be sexually harassed by male colleagues or service users.

- Women may face sexual harassment from water company staff when they register for household connections to new water sources.

- Workers may target women collecting water from community water sources, or female workers accessing campsite latrines at night.

D. Health

While health care services and centers can support SEAH prevention and response efforts, they can also be spaces where SEAH is perpetrated by and against health care workers, patients, and other service users. Health care workers have direct contact with and access to vulnerable patients, such as children, often in confined private spaces (such as hospital rooms), which presents SEAH risks. Examples of SEAH risks are as follows:

- Because of rapid expansion, hospital staff may be inadequately vetted and some staff who have previously been dismissed for perpetrating SEAH may be rehired.

- Construction workers on hospital sites may sexually harass young female visitors.

- Male doctors may use their position of power to sexually harass female patients or medical staff who are in a more junior position.

- Health care workers may target trans people and threaten them with disclosure about their transition to the community and/or withhold medical support in exchange for sex.

E.   Education

SEAH risks relating to education projects can occur inside and outside the classroom, around the education facilities (including those under construction), and on the way to and from the facility site. They can occur in primary, secondary, and tertiary education settings and in the education workforce. Students and construction workers can be survivors and perpetrators. Risks are greater in areas such as toilets, changing rooms, dormitories, corridors, and playgrounds, where students are less easily seen or supervised by school staff. If construction work (such as refurbishments or construction of new classrooms or construction of a new road) is taking place in and around the school, construction risks also apply and can take different forms (section A). Examples are as follows:

- Construction workers may perpetrate SEAH against girls, boys, or teachers while working on school construction sites. This may occur through exploitative "sugar daddy"[1] relationships between mobile workers with incomes and girls and women of school or university age.

- Teachers may perpetrate SEAH against students, particularly vulnerable students (such as those from minority ethnic groups, poor and vulnerable households, or students with disabilities) in exchange for grades.

- Project staff may ask for sexual favors in exchange for access to scholarships and grants funded by the project.

---

[1]   Usually, a rich older man who lavishes gifts on a young woman in return for her company or sexual favors.

Executing Agency and/or Implementing Agency Sexual Exploitation, Abuse, and Harassment: Self-Assessment Tool

Purpose of this tool. The purpose of this self-assessment tool is to support executing and implementing agencies in identifying any gaps in their capacity to deliver sexual exploitation, abuse, and harassment (SEAH) due diligence with contractors and to monitor contractors' SEAH delivery on an ongoing basis. This tool is not designed to assess the executing and implementing agencies' own SEAH systems and processes. The Asian Development Bank (ADB) has developed ADB SEAH minimum good practice standards (MGPS) that accompany the ADB's *Good Practice Note (GPN) on Addressing Sexual Exploitation, Abuse, and Harassment in ADB-Financed Projects with Civil Works.*

The executing and implementing agencies should use this tool to assess their needs with regards to being able to

1.   deliver the effective due diligence of contractors on addressing SEAH;
2.   monitor the implementation of the MGPS by contractors; and
3.   put in place provisions for the appropriate set-up and oversight of response mechanisms.

The executing and implementing agencies should use this tool to identify any gaps they have with regards to being able to

1.   review contractors' self-assessment to check it is adequate;
2.   review contractors' action plan to check it is adequate;
3.   provide advice, support, and capacity-building to the contractor to achieve their actions;
4.   monitor and support SEAH responses to SEAH concerns in contractor and its subcontractors and suppliers; and
5.   ensure SEAH reports made by the contractor to the executing and implementing agencies get to ADB.

Instructions. The executing and implementing agencies should

1.   read the due diligence section in the GPN;
2.   assess their capacity on addressing SEAH using MGPS/Priority Standards and identify any gaps they may have in terms of how they will review and monitor contractors' compliance with standards;
3.   reflect on any support needs that may be required, and use the key question/s as starting points;
4.   for substantial- and high-risk projects, the content of submissions from the contractor should be assessed in addition to checking if the policies, practices, and procedures aligned to the minimum good practice standards are present; and
5.   work with ADB (if needed) to review gaps and input activities to address those gaps in the action plan section of the tool, including associated costs (Annex F-2).

Self-Assessment Tool

Executing Agency/ Implementing Agency:		Date:	

I. Reflection on the capacity to conduct SEAH due diligence and monitoring of the MGPS implementation by contractors

Minimum Good Practice Standards for Contractor	Assessment and Reflections on Support Needs
Section A: SEAH Policy/ies	
Standard 1: Have a policy or a combination of relevant policies that address SEAH in the workplace and in the community.	(a) *Provide assessment of executing and implementing agencies' capacity with regard to meeting this standard, including identification of gaps.*
	(b) *Reflect on any support needs that may be required, e.g., do you feel able to support the contractor in SEAH policy work? For higher risk projects, this includes the content of the policy.*
Section B: Code of conduct	
Standard 2: Have a clear employee code of conduct that prohibits all forms of SEAH.	(a) *Provide assessment of executing and implementing agencies' capacity with regards to meeting this standard, including identification of gaps.*
	(b) *Reflect on any support needs that may be required, e.g., reflect on your capacity to review and provide support to contractors to develop content of the code of conduct. For higher risk projects, this includes the content of the code of conduct.*
Section C: Reporting, handling complaints, and whistleblowing (Priority standard) [1]	
Standard 3: Have or be willing to develop a comprehensive and confidential SEAH reporting mechanism for escalating and managing concerns and complaints. These should include the option of anonymous reporting and whistleblowing. These must be accessible to workers and community members who come into contact with contractors.	(a) *Provide assessment of executing and implementing agencies' capacity with regards to meeting this standard, including identification of gaps.*
	(b) *Reflect on any support needs that may be required, e.g., reflect on your capacity to review and provide support to the contractor to develop an appropriate reporting mechanism. This needs to include both a grievance and whistleblowing reporting process for staff, and a community reporting mechanism for community members involved in the project.*

continued on next page

---

[1] Standards 4–9 may be outsourced to an appropriate, specialized partner, which is recommended for substantial- and high-risk projects.

continued from previous page

Minimum Good Practice Standards for Contractor	Assessment and Reflections on Support Needs
Standard 4: Be able to work with communities and constituencies to analyze the most appropriate and accessible means to report concerns and complaints. Multiple methods to do so must be put in place.	(a) *Provide assessment of executing and implementing agencies' capacity with regards to meeting this standard, including identification of gaps.*
	(b) *Reflect on any support needs that may be required, e.g., reflect on your capacity to review and provide support to the contractor to develop an appropriate reporting mechanism. This needs to include both a grievance and whistleblowing reporting process for staff, and a community reporting mechanism for community members involved in the project.*
Standard 5: Be able to promote reporting mechanisms on the code of conduct to the staff and the community/ies in the project area.	(a) *Provide assessment of executing and implementing agencies' capacity with regards to meeting this standard, including identification of gaps.*
	(b) *Reflect on any support needs that may be required, e.g., contractors will need to be able to promote awareness and understanding of acceptable and unacceptable behaviors in the code of conduct to staff and community members. This is to ensure all are clear on expectations and are therefore more informed of their rights and what to report on. Contractors should be able to demonstrate a plan on how they will achieve this, which should include how they will work with community members to establish the most appropriate means of doing this.*
Standard 6: Have a clear internal handling framework to respond appropriately to all concerns and support the survivor in a survivor–centered way.	(a) *Provide assessment of executing and implementing agencies' capacity with regard to meeting this standard, including identification of gaps.*
	(b) *Reflect on any support needs that may be required, e.g., contractors will need to demonstrate their process for responding to SEAH concerns. This includes being able to demonstrate an understanding of a survivor-centered approach and how to put this in practice.*
Standard 7: Have identified and risk-assessed services available within the project context to ensure safe referrals of survivors can take place.	(a) *Provide assessment of executing and implementing agencies' capacity with regard to meeting this standard, including identification of gaps.*
	(b) *Reflect on any support needs that may be required, e.g., a basic service mapping report will be required for all projects and a more thorough service mapping report will be required for substantial- and high-risk projects. Reflect on your capacity to review this and support the contractor to achieve an acceptable service mapping for its project.*

continued on next page

continued from previous page

Minimum Good Practice Standards for Contractor	Assessment and Reflections on Support Needs
Standard 8: Have in-house trained investigators or have identified an appropriate external investigation resource.	(a) *Provide assessment of executing and implementing agencies' capacity with regard to meeting this standard, including identification of gaps.*
	(b) *Reflect on any support needs that may be required, e.g., reflect on your knowledge on SEAH investigation techniques and knowledge of local investigators.*
Standard 9: Have a whistleblowing policy that includes SEAH within it.	(a) *Provide assessment of executing and implementing agencies' capacity with regard to meeting this standard, including identification of gaps.*
	(b) *Reflect on any support needs that may be required, e.g., reflect on your capacity to review a contractor's whistleblowing policy.*
Section D: Human Resources	
Standard 10: All staff, contractors, volunteers, and other representatives have at least a mandatory induction training when they start and annual refresher training on the organization's SEAH policy and whistleblowing policy.	(a) *Provide assessment of executing and implementing agencies' capacity with regard to meeting this standard, including identification of gaps.*
	(b) *Reflect on any support needs that may be required, e.g., contractors need to demonstrate that this is provided. Executing and implementing agencies will need to check that the content is of a standard that they feel comfortable with for higher-risk projects.*
Standard 11: A recruitment approach that includes specific interview questions that draw out people's attitudes and values in relation to at-risk groups.	(a) *Provide assessment of executing and implementing agencies' capacity with regard to meeting this standard, including identification of gaps.*
	(b) *Reflect on any support needs that may be required, e.g., SEAH is based on abuse of power. Recruitment should factor this in and seek to ensure that values of candidates are clarified wherever possible.* **Police and background checks should be conducted for personnel who will engage with children or particularly at-risk adults.*

continued on next page

continued from previous page

Minimum Good Practice Standards for Contractor	Assessment and Reflections on Support Needs
Section E: Risk Management (Priority standard)	
Standard 12: Have a comprehensive and effective risk management framework in place that includes reference to SEAH and a detailed risk register for the project.	(a) *Provide assessment of executing and implementing agencies' capacity with regard to meeting this standard, including identification of gaps.*
	(b) *Reflect on any support needs that may be required, e.g., contractors need to provide an SEAH risk register for case management of substantial- and high-risk projects. Reflect on your capacity to review the framework.*
Standard 13: Have a detailed register of SEAH issues raised and how they were dealt with should be confidentially kept.	(a) *Provide assessment of executing and implementing agencies' capacity with regard to meeting this standard, including identification of gaps.*
	(b) *Reflect on any support needs that may be required, e.g., protecting data requires ethical, efficient collection of information that respects the complainant's privacy, confidentiality, safety, security, and wellbeing, and their ability to control their own information.*
Section F: Working with subcontractors and suppliers	
Standard 14: Include information on SEAH risks and expectations in contracts.	(a) *Provide assessment of executing and implementing agencies' capacity with regard to meeting this standard, including identification of gaps.*
	(b) *Reflect on any support needs that may be required, e.g., (i) reflect on the contractor's capacity to support their subcontractors and suppliers to meet this standard; (ii) ensure contracts with contractors include the requirement to integrate MGPS requirements and set out a monitoring schedule with dedicated staff member or team to oversee this work.*
Standard 15: Review subcontractors' policies against these minimum standards or similar. Where subcontractors do not have policies, practices, and procedures in place, subcontractors and suppliers should adhere to the contracting agencies' codes of conduct.	(a) *Provide assessment of executing and implementing agencies' capacity with regard to meeting this standard, including identification of gaps.*
	(b) *Reflect on any support needs that may be required, e.g., (i) reflect on the contractor's capacity to support their subcontractors and suppliers to meet this standard; (ii) reflect on capacity to ensure contractor is meeting this standard. The contractor should demonstrate the process and that these standards are being used and that subcontractors without are signing up to contractor policies. Ensure this is included in subcontractors' contracts; (iii) for substantial- and high-risk projects, a further detailed analysis of the content of the process and a sample analysis of subcontractor policies may be required.*

continued on next page

continued from previous page

Minimum Good Practice Standards for Contractor	Assessment and Reflections on Support Needs
Standard 16: Inform contractors and suppliers about project reporting mechanisms and the need to ensure these are in place.	(a) *Provide assessment of executing and implementing agencies' capacity with regard to meeting this standard, including identification of gaps.*
	(b) *Reflect on any support needs that may be required, e.g., reflect on the contractor's capacity to support their subcontractors and suppliers to meet this standard.*
Section G: Workplace Design	
Standard 17: Include SEAH in regular workplace safety assessments, including working accommodation, transportation, and site safety.	(a) *Provide assessment of executing and implementing agencies' capacity with regard to meeting this standard, including identification of gaps.*
	(b) *Reflect on any support needs that may be required, e.g., ensure executing and implementing agencies' dedicated staff are furnished with adequate information to review contractor workplace safety assessments, including requirements for SEAH prevention measures.*
Section H: Leadership and Accountability (Priority standard)	
Standard 18: Communication from the leadership of the contractor regarding its zero tolerance toward SEAH should occur regularly and utilize internal and external communication routes.	(a) *Provide assessment of executing and implementing agencies' capacity with regard to meeting this standard, including identification of gaps.*
	(b) *Reflect on any support needs that may be required, e.g., (i) contractors should provide evidence on how they have communicated this, e.g., e-mails, meeting minutes, posters, and leaflets; (ii) for substantial- and high-risk projects, also ensure this is included in contractor's SEAH policy review as a statement and in assessment of the contractor's processes for ensuring a communications plan.*
Standard 19: Have clear guidelines for monitoring and overseeing implementation of the policy/ies.	(a) *Provide assessment of executing and implementing agencies' capacity with regard to meeting this standard, including identification of gaps.*
	(b) *Reflect on any support needs that may be required, e.g., assess contractor's monitoring of subcontractors.*

continued on next page

continued from previous page

Minimum Good Practice Standards for Contractor	Assessment and Reflections on Support Needs
Standard 20: Have the capacity to report allegations to the executing and implementing agencies within 24 hours.	(a) *Provide assessment of executing and implementing agencies' capacity with regard to meeting this standard, including identification of gaps.*
	(b) *Reflect on any support needs that may be required, e.g., (i) contractor should have the capacity and ability to do this, including with their subcontractors; and (ii) contractors should have dedicated and trained focal points, accessible information provided to all, a relevant and accessible reporting mechanism, a communication plan for staff and community members that details how and what to report, and a dedicated e-mail and/or phone line.*

II. Reflection on capacity to engage on executing and implementing agency actions on SEAH throughout the project

Expectations per SEAH GPN	Reflections for Executing and Implementing Agencies[2]
Ability to oversee SEAH prevention, response, and mitigation throughout the life of the project	
a. Executing and implementing agencies should be able to oversee and support contractors in their case handling.	(a) *Provide assessment of executing and implementing agencies' capacity with regard to meeting this standard, including identification of gaps.*
	(b) *Reflect on any support needs that may be required, e.g.,* *(i) reflect on whether the executing and implementing agencies have the capacity to review and monitor contractor's ability to handle cases,* *(ii) reflect on whether the executing and implementing agencies have an appropriate system to hold case handling data, and* *(iii) reflect on whether executing and implementing agencies will be able to understand if the contractor is not handling the case according to minimum standards.*
b. Executing and implementing agencies should be able to receive and safely handle whistleblowing cases.	(a) *Provide assessment of executing and implementing agencies' capacity with regard to meeting this standard, including identification of gaps.*
	(b) *Reflect on any support needs that may be required, e.g., executing and implementing agencies may consider having* *(i) dedicated and trained focal points,* *(ii) provide accessible information to all,* *(iii) a relevant and accessible reporting mechanism,* *(iv) a communication plan for staff and community members of how and what to report, and* *(v) a dedicated e-mail and/or phone line.*

continued on next page

---

[2] For substantial- and high-risk projects the content of submissions from the contractor should be assessed in addition to checking if the policies, practices, and procedure aligned with the MGPS are present.

continued from previous page

Expectations per SEAH GPN	Reflections for Executing and Implementing Agencies[2]
c. Executing and implementing agencies should be able to monitor contractor's SEAH prevention, mitigation, and response in line with the MGPS.	(a) *Provide assessment of executing and implementing agencies' capacity with regard to meeting this standard, including identification of gaps.*
	(b) *Reflect on any support needs that may be required.*

III. Useful Resources

Standards	Tools That May Be Useful
1	*BOND safeguarding policy templates: https://www.bond.org.uk/resources/safeguarding-policy-templates. *British Council's writing safeguarding policy guidance: https://www.britishcouncil.org/sites/default/files/guide_safeguarding_policy.doc.
2	*ADB provides further detail of what should be included in a code of conduct on SEAH here (Annex H)
3	*Further details on reporting mechanism can be found in the SEAH GPN and in more detail in the GPN on SEAH Grievance Redress Mechanisms.
4	*A sample reporting form can be found here (Annex N) . This is for executing and implementing agencies, and can be also provided to contractors as a template to review and/or amend according to their needs. *Inter-Agency Standing Committee Best Practice Guide on Community Based Complaints Mechanisms. https://interagencystandingcommittee.org/iasc-task-team-accountability-affected-populations-and-protection-sexual-exploitation-and-abuse/iasc-best-practice-guide-inter-agency-community-based-complaints-mechanisms-2016. *CHS Alliance PSEAH Implementation Quick Reference Handbook, Engaging Communities and People Affected by Crisis. https://www.chsalliance.org/get-support/resource/pseah-implementation-quick-reference-handbook/.
5	* Further details on reporting mechanism can be found in the SEAH GPN and in more detail in the GPN on SEAH Grievance Redress Mechanisms.
6	* Further details on reporting mechanism can be found in the SEAH GPN and in more detail in the GPN on SEAH Grievance Redress Mechanisms. * A sample reporting form can be found here. This is for executing and implementing agencies, and can be also provided to contractors as a template to review and/or amend according to their needs. * Inter-Agency Standing Committee Best Practice Guide on Community Based Complaints Mechanisms https://interagencystandingcommittee.org/iasc-task-team-accountability-affected-populations-and-protection-sexual-exploitation-and-abuse/iasc-best-practice-guide-inter-agency-community-based-complaints-mechanisms-2016. * CHS Alliance PSEAH Implementation Quick Reference Handbook, Engaing Communities and People Affected by Crisis https://www.chsalliance.org/get-support/resource/pseah-implementation-quick-reference-handbook/.
7	* ADB's service mapping tool is available here (Annex I) .
8	* CHS guidelines for investigations https://www.chsalliance.org/get-support/resource/sexual-exploitation-abuse-and-harassment-seah-investigation-guide/.
9	* Further details on the reporting mechanism can be found in the SEAH GPN and in more detail in the GPN on SEAH Grievance Redress Mechanisms. * A sample incidents reporting templates can be found here (Annex N). * Inter-Agency Standing Committee Best Practice Guide on Community Based Complaints Mechanisms https://interagencystandingcommittee.org/iasc-task-team-accountability-affected-populations-and-protection-sexual-exploitation-and-abuse/iasc-best-practice-guide-inter-agency-community-based-complaints-mechanisms-2016. * CHS Alliance PSEAH Implementation Quick Reference Handbook, Engaging Communities and People Affected by Crisis. https://www.chsalliance.org/get-support/resource/pseah-implementation-quick-reference-handbook/.

continued on next page

continued from previous page

Standards	Tools That May Be Useful
10	* Resource and Support Hub training materials: https://safeguardingsupporthub.org/learning.
11	* The Inter-Agency Standing Committee's Challenges and Options in Improving Recruitment Process in the Context of PSEAH by Our Own Staff. https://interagencystandingcommittee.org/accountability-affected-populations-including-protection-sexual-exploitation-and-abuse/documents-3. * British Council's International Criminal Records Check Directory: https://www.britishcouncil.org/sites/default/files/international_criminal_record_checks_directory.xls. * International Rescue Committee's, Caring for Child Survivors Attitude Scale https://gbvresponders.org/wp-content/uploads/2014/07/2_CCS-Attitude-Scale.pdf. * International Rescue Committee GBV Blended Curriculum, in particular the section on attitudes https://gbvresponders.org/gbv-blended-curriculum/#CurriculumModules.
12	* National Council for Voluntary Action Risk Management Guidance https://knowhow.ncvo.org.uk/safeguarding/checklists-training-and-other-support/specialist-guides/safeguarding-as-a-director-of-operations/managing-safeguarding-risks. * The Inter-Agency Standing Committee GBV Guidelines: https://gbvguidelines.org/en/. * The UN Department of Field Support Sexual Exploitation and Abuse Risk Management Toolkit: https://conduct.unmissions.org/sites/default/files/dpko-dfs_sea_risk_toolkit_28_june_2018_modified.pdf. * The Australian Government Department of Foreign Affairs and Trade PSEAH Risk Guidance Note and Child Protection Guidance Note on Establishing Child Protection Risk Context: https://safeguardingsupporthub.org/documents/dfat-child-protection-guidance-note-establishing-child-protection-risk-context.
13	* Inter-agency Gender-Based Violence Case Management Guidelines. Providing Care and Case Management Services to Gender-Based Violence Survivors in Humanitarian Settings, First Edition, 2017, p. 179: http://www.gbvims.com/wp/wp-content/uploads/Interagency-GBV-Case-Management-Guidelines_Final_2017.pdf.
14	See relevant tools throughout this publication.
15	See relevant tools throughout this publication.
16	See relevant tools throughout this publication.
17	* ActionAid and Social Development Direct's Safety Audit Participatory Toolkit: https://cambodia.actionaid.org/sites/cambodia/files/actionaid_safety_audit_participatory_toolkit.pdf.
18	NA
19	* Monitoring guidance in Annex L can be adapted for use by executing agencies, implementing agencies, and contractors.
20	* All tools above are relevant.
a	* See tools under area C above.
b	* See tools under area C above .
c	* Monitoring guidance can be adapted for use by executing agencies, implementing agencies, and contractors. * Comprehensive monitoring tools can be downloaded and adapted from the Girls' Education Challenge: Non-specialist monitoring: https://girlseducationchallenge.org/media/hkimvcif/14montool-not-to-be-designed.pdf. Safety audit: https://girlseducationchallenge.org/media/k45dbbt3/15montool-not-to-be-designed.pdf. Monitoring policy and compliance issues: https://girlseducationchallenge.org/media/ad2mveaj/20montool-not-to-be-designed.pdf. Monitoring culture, enabling environment, and implementation of Prevention of Sexual Exploitation and Abuse work: https://girlseducationchallenge.org/media/g1jktvu1/18montool-not-to-be-designed.pdf.

Executing Agency and/or Implementing Agency Sexual Exploitation, Abuse, and Harassment: Action Plan Template

Purpose of this tool. The purpose of this tool is to support executing and implementing agencies in planning actions to address SEAH in ADB-financed projects with civil works.

Instructions. The executing and/or implementing agencies should

1. read the due diligence section in the good practice note (GPN);
2. based on findings and results of using self-assessment tool (Annex F-1), work with ADB (if needed) to review gaps and identify outputs and activities to address these gaps; and
3. input the outputs and activities, including associated costs, in spaces provided in the action plan template.

Template for Action Plan

Executing Agency/ Implementing Agency:		Date:	

Areas Identified for Strengthening	Target Output/s	Timeline and Completion Date	Person and Unit Responsible	Budget or Estimated Cost
Capacity to conduct SEAH due diligence with and monitoring of the MGPS implementation by contractors				
Section A: SEAH Policy/ies (Priority standard)				
Standard 1: Have a policy or a combination of relevant policies that address SEAH in the workplace and in the community				
Section B: Code of conduct (Priority standard)				
Standard 2: Have a clear employee code of conduct that prohibits all forms of SEAH				
Section C: Reporting, handling complaints, and whistleblowing (Priority standard)				
Standard 3: Have or be willing to develop a comprehensive and confidential SEAH reporting mechanism for escalating and managing concerns and complaints				
Standard 4: Be able to work with communities and constituencies to analyze the most appropriate and accessible means to report concerns and complaints				

continued on next page

continued from previous page

Areas Identified for Strengthening	Target Output/s	Timeline and Completion Date	Person and Unit Responsible	Budget or Estimated Cost
Standard 5: Be able to promote reporting mechanisms on the code of conduct to the staff and the community/ies in the project area				
Standard 6: Have a clear internal handling framework to respond appropriately to all concerns and support the survivor in a survivor-centered way				
Standard 7: Have identified and risk assessed services available within the project context to ensure safe referrals of survivors can take place				
Standard 8: Have in-house trained investigators or have identified an appropriate external investigation resource				
Standard 9: Have a whistleblowing policy that includes SEAH within it				
Section D: Human Resources				
Standard 10: All staff, contractors, volunteers, and other representatives have at least a mandatory induction training when they start and annual refresher training on the organization's SEAH policy and whistleblowing policy				
Standard 11: A recruitment approach that includes specific interview questions that draw out people's attitudes and values in relation to at-risk groups				
Section E: Risk Management (Priority standard)				
Standard 12: Have a comprehensive and effective risk management framework in place that includes reference to SEAH and a detailed risk register for the project				
Standard 13: Have a detailed register of SEAH issues raised and how they were dealt with should be confidentially kept				

continued on next page

continued from previous page

Areas Identified for Strengthening	Target Output/s	Timeline and Completion Date	Person and Unit Responsible	Budget or Estimated Cost
Section F: Working with subcontractors and suppliers				
Standard 14: Include information on SEAH risks and expectations in contracts				
Standard 15: Review subcontractors' policies against these minimum standards or similar				
Standard 16: Inform contractors and suppliers about project reporting mechanisms and the need to ensure these are in place				
Section G: Workplace Design				
Standard 17: Include SEAH in regular workplace safety assessments, including working accommodation, transportation, and site safety				
Section H: Leadership and Accountability (Priority standard)				
Standard 18: Communication from the leadership of the contractor regarding its zero tolerance toward SEAH should occur regularly and utilize internal and external communication routes				
Standard 19: Have clear guidelines for monitoring and overseeing implementation of the policy or policies				
Standard 20: Have the capacity to report allegations to the executing and implementing agencies within 24 hours				

Oversight of SEAH prevention, mitigation and response throughout the life of the project				
a. Executing and implementing agencies should be able to oversee and support contractors in their case handling				
b. Executing and implementing agencies should be able to receive and safely handle whistleblowing cases				
c. Executing and implementing agencies should be able to monitor contractor's SEAH prevention, mitigation, and response in line with the MGPS				

Minimum Good Practice Standards Due Diligence and Sexual Exploitation, Abuse, and Harassment: Self-Assessment Template

Purpose of this tool. As part of the due diligence processes and preparation for bidding, all bidders are asked to fill in the below self-assessment form to assess their level of compliance with the Minimum Good Practice Standards (MGPS). These standards should be seen as the minimum and contractors are encouraged to go beyond them during the course of project implementation.

Based on this self-assessment, bidders will need to develop a sexual exploitation, abuse, and harassment (SEAH) action plan to set out their actions to meet the gaps identified in this self-assessment (Annex G-2).

Instructions:

The contractor should (Table I - Assessment)

1. fill in their responses as to how they are currently meeting the standards and provide evidence for the executing and implementing agencies reviewer;
2. provide documents they refer to in their response;
3. if any, provide information on anticipated support or assistance from executing and implementing agencies; and
4. use Red, Amber, Green (RAG) rate if they feel they have met, partially met, or not met each standard.

If the contractor has any questions or requires further support or information to complete the assessment, they should notify their ADB contact.

The executing and implementing agencies reviewer should (Table II - Rating)

1. read the contractors response and add their comments and guidance using the guidance information in the executing and implementing agencies self-assessment tool; and
2. RAG rate whether the contractor has met, partially met, or not met each standard:

    RED – Standard not met

    AMBER – Standard partly met but still needs further work

    GREEN – Standard satisfactorily met

Template for Minimum Good Practice Standards Compliance Self-Assessment for Contractors

| Contractor Name: | | Date: | |

I. Assessment

Key Questions	Response: Assessment and Anticipated Support Needs
Section A: SEAH Policy/ies (Priority standard)	
Standard 1: Have a policy or a combination of relevant policies which address SEAH in the workplace and in the community	
Does the policy or combination of policies include a statement of your commitment to SEAH, including a zero-tolerance statement targeted at both staff and community members of the project?	(a) *Provide information showing how this has been met.*
	(b) *Evidence of compliance - provide link to relevant documents.*
	(c) *If any, provide information on anticipated support or assistance from executing and implementing agencies.*
Does it set out how to report SEAH concerns?	(a) *Provide information showing how this has been met.*
	(b) *Evidence of compliance - provide link to relevant documents.*
	(c) *If any, provide information on anticipated support or assistance from executing and implementing agencies.*
Does the policy set out requirements in relation to consent? If so, please outline.	(a) *Provide information showing how this has been met.*
	(b) *Evidence of compliance - provide link to relevant documents.*
	(c) *If any, provide information on anticipated support or assistance from executing and implementing agencies.*
Does the policy set out requirements in relation to data protection? If so, please outline.	(a) *Provide information showing how this has been met.*
	(b) *Evidence of compliance - provide link to relevant documents.*
	(c) *If any, provide information on anticipated support or assistance from executing and implementing agencies.*
Section B: Code of Conduct (Priority standard)	
Standard 2: Have a clear employee code of conduct which prohibits all forms of SEAH	
Does your code of conduct apply to staff and volunteers inside and outside the work place? What will happen in the event of noncompliance or breach of these standards?	(a) *Provide information showing how this has been met.*
	(b) *Evidence of compliance - provide link to relevant documents.*
	(c) *If any, provide information on anticipated support or assistance from executing and implementing agencies.*

continued on next page

continued from previous page

Key Questions	Response: Assessment and Anticipated Support Needs
Does your code of conduct link with existing national and local legislation in the country/countries where your project will work? If so, how?	(a) *Provide information showing how this has been met.*
	(b) *Evidence of compliance - provide link to relevant documents.*
	(c) *If any, provide information on anticipated support or assistance from executing and implementing agencies.*
Does your code of conduct comply with the Asian Development Bank's (ADB) SEAH good practice note (GPN) Annex H Code of Conduct?	(a) *Provide information showing how this has been met.*
	(b) *Evidence of compliance - provide link to relevant documents.*
	(c) *If any, provide information on anticipated support or assistance from executing and implementing agencies.*

Section C: Reporting, handling complaints, and whistleblowing (Priority standard)

Standard 3: Have or be willing to develop a comprehensive and confidential SEAH reporting mechanism for escalating and managing concerns and complaints

Describe your SEAH reporting mechanism and how you ensure it is confidential and whether it includes anonymous reporting options	(a) *Provide information showing how this has been met.*
	(b) *Evidence of compliance - provide link to relevant documents.*
	(c) *If any, provide information on anticipated support or assistance from executing and implementing agencies.*
Describe how your SEAH reporting mechanism is accessible to all staff/employees, including those on temporary engagement and community members in the project	(a) *Provide information showing how this has been met.*
	(b) *Evidence of compliance - provide link to relevant documents.*
	(c) *If any, provide information on anticipated support or assistance from executing and implementing agencies.*

Standard 4: Be able to work with communities and constituencies to analyze the most appropriate and accessible means to report concerns and complaints

How do you involve communities/constituencies in gaining their views and inputs into reporting mechanisms?	(a) *Provide information showing how this has been met.*
	(b) *Evidence of compliance - provide link to relevant documents.*
	(c) *If any, provide information on anticipated support or assistance from executing and implementing agencies.*

Standard 5: Be able to promote reporting mechanisms on the code of conduct to the staff and the community/ies in the project area

How do you promote reporting mechanisms to staff?	(a) *Provide information showing how this has been met.*
	(b) *Evidence of compliance - provide link to relevant documents.*
	(c) *If any, provide information on anticipated support or assistance from executing and implementing agencies.*

continued on next page

continued from previous page

Key Questions	Response: Assessment and Anticipated Support Needs
How do you promote reporting mechanisms to residents and community members residing in the project area?	(a) *Provide information showing how this has been met.*
	(b) *Evidence of compliance - provide link to relevant documents.*
	(c) *If any, provide information on anticipated support or assistance from executing and implementing agencies.*
Standard 6: Have a clear internal handling framework to respond appropriately to all concerns and support the survivor in a survivor-centred way	
Describe your internal handling framework. Do you have standard operational procedures for case handling?	(a) *Provide information showing how this has been met.*
	(b) *Evidence of compliance - provide link to relevant documents.*
	(c) *If any, provide information on anticipated support or assistance from executing and implementing agencies.*
Standard 7: Have identified and risk assessed services available within the project context to ensure safe referrals of survivors can take place	
How do you identify and risk assess services for safe referrals of survivors?	(a) *Provide information showing how this has been met.*
	(b) *Evidence of compliance - provide link to relevant documents.*
	(c) *If any, provide information on anticipated support or assistance from executing and implementing agencies.*
Standard 8: Have in-house trained investigators or have identified an appropriate external investigation resource	
Do you have in-house trained investigators? What training have they received?	(a) *Provide information showing how this has been met.*
	(b) *Evidence of compliance - provide link to relevant documents.*
	(c) *If any, provide information on anticipated support or assistance from executing and implementing agencies.*
Do you have a vetted external investigation resource?	(a) *Provide information showing how this has been met.*
	(b) *Evidence of compliance - provide link to relevant documents.*
	(c) *If any, provide information on anticipated support or assistance from executing and implementing agencies.*
Are you aware of and do you follow the Core Humanitarian Standards Investigations guidance?	(a) *Provide information showing how this has been met.*
	(b) *Evidence of compliance - provide link to relevant documents.*
	(c) *If any, provide information on anticipated support or assistance from executing and implementing agencies.*

continued on next page

continued from previous page

Key Questions	Response: Assessment and Anticipated Support Needs
Standard 9: Have a whistleblowing policy that includes SEAH within it	
Does your whistleblowing policy explicitly refer to SEAH?	(a) *Provide information showing how this has been met.*
	(b) *Evidence of compliance - provide link to relevant documents.*
	(c) *If any, provide information on anticipated support or assistance from executing and implementing agencies.*
Does your whistleblowing policy and procedure outline clear processes for dealing with concerns raised? If so, by whom? What are the timelines involved?	(a) *Provide information showing how this has been met.*
	(b) *Evidence of compliance - provide link to relevant documents.*
	(c) *If any, provide information on anticipated support or assistance from executing and implementing agencies.*
Does your whistleblowing policy set out confidentiality measures and a commitment to protection from reprisals?	(a) *Provide information showing how this has been met.*
	(b) *Evidence of compliance - provide link to relevant documents.*
	(c) *If any, provide information on anticipated support or assistance from executing and implementing agencies.*
Section D: Human Resources	
Standard 10: All staff, contractors, volunteers, and other representatives have at least a mandatory induction training when they start and annual refresher training on the organization's SEAH policy and whistleblowing policy	
What mandatory induction and annual refresher SEAH/whistleblowing training do you have?	(a) *Provide information showing how this has been met.*
	(b) *Evidence of compliance - provide link to relevant documents.*
	(c) *If any, provide information on anticipated support or assistance from executing and implementing agencies.*
How do you record staff attendance and assure all staff attend?	(a) *Provide information showing how this has been met.*
	(b) *Evidence of compliance - provide link to relevant documents.*
	(c) *If any, provide information on anticipated support or assistance from executing and implementing agencies.*
Standard 11: A recruitment approach that includes specific interview questions that draw out people's attitudes and values in relation to at-risk groups	
How do you ensure these specific interview questions are used in recruitment?	(a) *Provide information showing how this has been met.*
	(b) *Evidence of compliance - provide link to relevant documents.*
	(c) *If any, provide information on anticipated support or assistance from executing and implementing agencies.*

continued on next page

continued from previous page

Key Questions	Response: Assessment and Anticipated Support Needs
Section E: Risk Management (Priority standard)	
Standard 12: Have a comprehensive and effective risk management framework in place that includes reference to SEAH and a detailed risk register for the project	
Do you have a risk management policy or framework which captures SEAH risks?	*(a) Provide information showing how this has been met.*
	(b) Evidence of compliance - provide link to relevant documents.
	(c) If any, provide information on anticipated support or assistance from executing and implementing agencies.
Has your organization conducted an SEAH risk assessment of the proposed ADB activities? If yes, please give details SEAH mitigation actions you will put in place.	*(a) Provide information showing how this has been met.*
	(b) Evidence of compliance - provide link to relevant documents.
	(c) If any, provide information on anticipated support or assistance from executing and implementing agencies.
Standard 13: Have a detailed register of SEAH issues raised and how they were dealt with should be confidentially kept	
Do you have requirements for SEAH case register? What type of information and actions does the register include?	*(a) Provide information showing how this has been met.*
	(b) Evidence of compliance - provide link to relevant documents.
	(c) If any, provide information on anticipated support or assistance from executing and implementing agencies.
Are there clear requirements for confidentiality?	*(a) Provide information showing how this has been met.*
	(b) Evidence of compliance - provide link to relevant documents.
	(c) If any, provide information on anticipated support or assistance from executing and implementing agencies.
Section F: Working with subcontractors and suppliers	
Standard 14: Include information on SEAH risks and expectations in contracts	
Do you include information on SEAH risks/expectations in contracts?	*(a) Provide information showing how this has been met.*
	(b) Evidence of compliance - provide link to relevant documents.
	(c) If any, provide information on anticipated support or assistance from executing and implementing agencies.
How do you monitor SEAH risks and mitigation actions in the project with your subcontractors and suppliers?	*(a) Provide information showing how this has been met.*
	(b) Evidence of compliance - provide link to relevant documents.
	(c) If any, provide information on anticipated support or assistance from executing and implementing agencies.

continued on next page

continued from previous page

Key Questions	Response: Assessment and Anticipated Support Needs
Standard 15: Review subcontractors' policies against these minimum standards or similar	
What process do you use to audit subcontractors'/suppliers' SEAH measures?	(a) Provide information showing how this has been met.
	(b) Evidence of compliance - provide link to relevant documents.
	(c) If any, provide information on anticipated support or assistance from executing and implementing agencies.
What is your process where a subcontractor/supplier does not have appropriate SEAH policies, practices in place?	(a) Provide information showing how this has been met.
	(b) Evidence of compliance - provide link to relevant documents.
	(c) If any, provide information on anticipated support or assistance from executing and implementing agencies.
Standard 16: Inform contractors and suppliers about project reporting mechanisms and the need to ensure these are in place	
How do you ensure subcontractors/ suppliers understand the project reporting systems and have integrated them?	(a) Provide information showing how this has been met.
	(b) Evidence of compliance - provide link to relevant documents.
	(c) If any, provide information on anticipated support or assistance from executing and implementing agencies.
Section G: Workplace Design	
Standard 17: Include SEAH in regular workplace safety assessments, including working accommodation, transportation, and site safety	
How do you incorporate SEAH into your workplace safety assessments?	(a) Provide information showing how this has been met.
	(b) Evidence of compliance - provide link to relevant documents.
	(c) If any, provide information on anticipated support or assistance from executing and implementing agencies.
How do you monitor and review workplace safety assessments?	(a) Provide information showing how this has been met.
	(b) Evidence of compliance - provide link to relevant documents.
	(c) If any, provide information on anticipated support or assistance from executing and implementing agencies.
Section H: Leadership and Accountability (Priority standard)	
Standard 18: Communication from the leadership of the contractor regarding its zero tolerance toward SEAH should occur regularly and utilize internal and external communication routes	
How does leadership communicate SEAH zero tolerance to the workforce?	(a) Provide information showing how this has been met.
	(b) Evidence of compliance - provide link to relevant documents.
	(c) If any, provide information on anticipated support or assistance from executing and implementing agencies.

continued on next page

continued from previous page

Key Questions	Response: Assessment and Anticipated Support Needs
Standard 19: Have clear guidelines for monitoring and overseeing implementation of the policy or policies	
What is your process for monitoring implementation of SEAH policies?	(a) *Provide information showing how this has been met.*
	(b) *Evidence of compliance – provide link to relevant documents.*
	(c) *If any, provide information on anticipated support or assistance from executing and implementing agencies.*
Standard 20: Have the capacity to report allegations to the executing and implementing agencies within 24 hours	
What processes and agreements are in place between you and your subcontractors/suppliers to report SEAH concerns and for this information to be shared with executing and implementing agencies in a timely manner?	(a) *Provide information showing how this has been met.*
	(b) *Evidence of compliance – provide link to relevant documents.*
	(c) *If any, provide information on anticipated support or assistance from executing and implementing agencies.*
Do you have a person or persons tasked with reporting any arising SEAH breaches to the ADB? If so, who?	(a) *Provide information showing how this has been met.*
	(b) *Evidence of compliance – provide link to relevant documents.*
	(c) *If any, provide information on anticipated support or assistance from executing and implementing agencies.*
Does the contractor have a person or team responsible for coordinating responses and action planning to investigate and address corrective action related to SEAH breaches? Explain their role.	(a) *Provide information showing how this has been met.*
	(b) *Evidence of compliance – provide link to relevant documents.*
	(c) *If any, provide information on anticipated support or assistance from executing and implementing agencies.*

II. Rating Assessment Results

Rating: SEAH Policy/ies (Priority standard)				
To be completed by contractor			To be completed by executing and implementing agencies	
Key Questions		Rating	Rating	Comments/Guidance
Section A: SEAH Policy/ies (Priority standard)				
Standard 1: Have a policy or a combination of relevant policies which address SEAH in the workplace and in the community				
Does the policy or combination of policies include a statement of your commitment to SEAH, including a zero-tolerance statement targeted at both staff and community members of the project?				
Does it set out how to report SEAH concerns?				
Does the policy set out requirements in relation to data protection? If so, please outline.				
Section B: Code of Conduct (Priority standard)				*continued on next page*

continued from previous page

Key Questions	Rating	Rating	Comments/Guidance
Standard 2: Have a clear employee code of conduct which prohibits all forms of SEAH			
Does your code of conduct apply to staff and volunteers inside and outside the work place? What will happen in the event of noncompliance or breach of these standards?			
Does your code of conduct link with existing national and local legislation in the country/countries where your project will work? If so, how?			
Does your code of conduct comply with ADB SEAH GPN Annex H Code of Conduct?			
Section C: Reporting, handling complaints, and whistleblowing (Priority standard)			
Standard 3: Have or be willing to develop a comprehensive and confidential SEAH reporting mechanism for escalating and managing concerns and complaints			
Describe your SEAH reporting mechanism and how you ensure it is confidential and whether it includes anonymous reporting options			
Describe how your SEAH reporting mechanism is accessible to all staff/employees, including those on temporary engagement and to community members in the project.			
Standard 4: Be able to work with communities and constituencies to analyze the most appropriate and accessible means to report concerns and complaints			
How do you involve communities/constituencies in gaining their views and inputs into reporting mechanisms?			
Standard 5: Be able to promote reporting mechanisms on the code of conduct to the staff and the community/ies in the project area			
How do you promote reporting mechanisms to staff?			
How do you promote reporting mechanisms to residents and community members residing in the project area?			
Standard 6: Have a clear internal handling framework to respond appropriately to all concerns and support the survivor in a survivor-centred way			
Describe your internal handling framework. Do you have standard operational procedures for case handling?			
Standard 7: Have identified and risk assessed services available within the project context to ensure safe referrals of survivors can take place			
How do you identify and risk assess services for safe referrals of survivors?			
Standard 8: Have in-house trained investigators or have identified an appropriate external investigation resource			
Do you have in-house trained investigators? What training have they received?			
Do you have a vetted external investigation resource?			
Are you aware of and do you follow the Core Humanitarian Standards Investigations guidance?			

continued on next page

continued from previous page

Key Questions	Rating	Rating	Comments/Guidance
Standard 9: Have a whistleblowing policy that includes SEAH within it			
Does your whistleblowing policy explicitly refer to SEAH?			
Does your whistleblowing policy and procedure outline clear processes for dealing with concerns raised? If so, by whom? What are the timelines involved?			
Does your whistleblowing policy set out confidentiality measures and a commitment to protection from reprisals?			
Section D: Human Resources			
Standard 10: All staff, contractors, volunteers, and other representatives have at least a mandatory induction training when they start and annual refresher training on the organization's SEAH policy and whistleblowing policy			
What mandatory induction and annual refresher SEAH/whistleblowing training do you have?			
How do you record staff attendance and assure all staff attend?			
Standard 11: A recruitment approach that includes specific interview questions that draw out people's attitudes and values in relation to at-risk groups			
How do you ensure these specific interview questions are used in recruitment?			
Section E: Risk Management (Priority standard)			
Standard 12: Have a comprehensive and effective risk management framework in place that includes reference to SEAH and a detailed risk register for the project			
Do you have a risk management policy or framework which captures SEAH risks?			
Has your organization conducted an SEAH risk assessment of the proposed ADB activities? If yes, please give details of SEAH mitigation actions you will put in place.			
Standard 13: Have a detailed register of SEAH issues raised and how they were dealt with should be confidentially kept			
Do you have requirements for SEAH case register? What type of information and actions does the register include?			
Are there clear requirements for confidentiality?			
Section F: Working with subcontractors and suppliers			
Standard 14: Include information on SEAH risks and expectations in contracts			
Do you include information on SEAH risks/expectations in contracts?			
How do you monitor SEAH risks and mitigation actions in the project with your subcontractors and suppliers?			
Standard 15: Review subcontractors' policies against these minimum standards or similar			
What process do you use to audit subcontractors/suppliers SEAH measures?			
What is your process where a subcontractor/supplier does not have appropriate SEAH policies, practices in place?			
Standard 16: Inform contractors and suppliers about project reporting mechanisms and the need to ensure these are in place			
How do you ensure subcontractors/suppliers understand the project reporting systems and have integrated them?			

continued on next page

continued from previous page

Key Questions	Rating	Rating	Comments/Guidance
Section G: Workplace Design			
Standard 17: Include SEAH in regular workplace safety assessments, including working accommodation, transportation, and site safety			
How do you incorporate SEAH into your workplace safety assessments?			
How do you monitor and review workplace safety assessments?			
Section H: Leadership and Accountability (Priority standard)			
Standard 18: Communication from the leadership of the contractor regarding its zero-tolerance toward SEAH should occur regularly and utilize internal and external communication routes			
How does leadership communicate SEAH zero tolerance to the workforce?			
Standard 19: Have clear guidelines for monitoring and overseeing implementation of the policy or policies			
What is your process for monitoring implementation of SEAH policies?			
Standard 20: Have the capacity to report allegations to the executing and implementing agencies within 24 hours			
What processes and agreements are in place between you and your subcontractors/suppliers to report SEAH concerns and for this information to be shared with executing and implementing agencies in a timely manner?			
Do you have a person or persons tasked with reporting any arising SEAH breaches to the ADB? If so, who?			
Does the contractor have a person or team responsible for coordinating responses and action planning to investigate and address corrective action related to SEAH breaches? Explain their role.			

ANNEX G-2
Minimum Good Practice Standards Due Diligence and Sexual Exploitation, Abuse, and Harassment: Action Plan Template

Purpose of this tool. This template guides prospective contractors in formulating a sexual exploitation, abuse, and harassment (SEAH) action plan. The SEAH action plan is required by the executing and implementing agencies from prospective contractors as part of the package of documents submitted during the bidding process. The contractor's SEAH action plan presents the activities and strategies, outputs, lead person and units, timeline, and cost estimate for addressing the gaps that have been identified earlier, including those found through the self-assessment. For projects classified substantial- and high-risk, it is expected that the coverage and scope of actions and targets will be more extensive compared with projects rated low or moderate risk.

Instructions. The contractor should perform the following

- Review the gaps identified from the SEAH self-assessment tool, service mapping, and SEAH analysis and in-depth assessment.

- Address the gaps through actions or strategies. See the minimum good practice standards-based actions and strategies provided as suggestions/examples on the second column of the SEAH action plan matrix below. These are just suggestions, i.e., identification of actions and strategies should always be in line with the gaps. Any actions that are not relevant may be deleted or language may be amended to fit the requirements of the project, i.e., add or delete, as applicable.

- Add the date by which you intend to complete the actions. Priority actions must be completed prior to the start of the project and all others should be completed within the first year.

The contractor's SEAH action plan will be attached to its contract with the executing and/or implementing agency. Tracking implementation of the action plan will be incorporated into the project monitoring system and as such, regular project progress reports should contain updates on achieving the actions in the contractors' SEAH action plans.

Template for Sexual Exploitation, Abuse, and Harassment Action Plan

Executing Agency/ Implementing Agency:		Date:	
Contractor		Date:	

Identified SEAH Gap	Identified Action or Strategies	Target Output/s	Timeline and Date to be Completed	Person and Unit Responsible	Budget or Estimated Cost
Section A: SEAH Policy/ies (Priority standard)					
Standard 1: Have a policy or a combination of relevant policies that address SEAH in the workplace and in the community					
	e.g., Review or develop policy to include a statement of your commitment to SEAH, including a zero-tolerance statement for SEAH targeted at staff and community members of the project.				
	e.g., Review or develop policy to include details on how to report SEAH concerns.				
	e.g., Review or develop policy to provide specific SEAH processes that need to be followed when conducting activities directly with children.				
	e.g., Review or develop policy to set out requirements in relation to consent and data protection.				
Section B: Code of conduct (Priority standard)					
Standard 2: Have a clear employee code of conduct that prohibits all forms of SEAH					
	e.g., Review or develop code of conduct to ensure that it applies to staff and volunteers, inside and outside the workplace, and details what will happen in the event of noncompliance or breach of these standards.				
	e.g., Review or develop code of conduct to ensure it links with existing national and local legislation in the country or countries where your project will work.				
	e.g., Review or develop code of conduct to ensure it complies with guidance.				
Section C: Reporting, handling complaints, and whistleblowing (Priority standard)					
Standard 3: Have or be willing to develop a comprehensive and confidential SEAH reporting mechanism for escalating and managing concerns and complaints					
	e.g., Review or develop reporting mechanism for staff that is accessible, confidential, and includes anonymous reporting options.				
	e.g., Review or develop a reporting mechanism for community members that is accessible, confidential, and includes anonymous reporting options.				

continued on next page

continued from previous page

Identified SEAH Gap	Identified Action or Strategies	Target Output/s	Timeline and Date to be Completed	Person and Unit Responsible	Budget or Estimated Cost
Standard 4: Be able to work with communities and constituencies to analyze the most appropriate and accessible means to report concerns and complaints					
	e.g., Develop a strategy for how you will work with communities or constituencies and provide evidence of the results.				
Standard 5: Be able to promote reporting mechanisms on the code of conduct to the staff and the community/ies in the project area					
	e.g., Develop a strategy for how you will promote reporting mechanisms to your staff and provide evidence of the actions when completed.				
	e.g., Develop a strategy for how you will promote reporting mechanisms to community members and provide evidence of the actions when completed.				
Standard 6: Have a clear internal handling framework to respond appropriately to all concerns and support the survivor in a survivor-centered way					
	e.g., Develop an internal handling framework and standard operating procedure for case handling.				
	e.g., Develop a document on how you ensure you support survivors of SEAH in a survivor centred way.				
Standard 7: Have identified and risk assessed services available within the project context to ensure safe referrals of survivors can take place					
	e.g., Develop a procedure for identifying and risk assessing services for safe referrals of survivors.				
Standard 8: Have in-house trained investigators or have identified an appropriate external investigation resource					
	e.g., Select staff to be trained as investigators and provide them with appropriate investigations training.				
	e.g., Develop a roster of vetted external investigators.				
Standard 9: Have a whistleblowing policy that includes SEAH within it					
	e.g., Review or develop a whistleblowing policy that includes explicit reference to SEAH.				
	e.g., Review or develop a whistleblowing policy and procedure that outlines clear processes for dealing with concerns raised, specifies who may raise the concerns, and the timelines involved.				

continued on next page

continued from previous page

Identified SEAH Gap	Identified Action or Strategies	Target Output/s	Timeline and Date to be Completed	Person and Unit Responsible	Budget or Estimated Cost
	e.g., Review or develop a whistleblowing policy to include confidentiality measures and a commitment to protection from reprisals.				
Section D: Human Resources					
Standard 10: All staff, contractors, volunteers, and other representatives have at least a mandatory induction training when they start and annual refresher training on the organization's SEAH policy and whistleblowing policy					
	e.g., Develop or provide evidence of mandatory induction and annual refresher SEAH and whistleblowing training.				
	e.g., Develop or provide evidence of how you record staff attendance and assure all staff attend induction and yearly training.				
Standard 11: A recruitment approach that includes specific interview questions that draw out people's attitudes and values in relation to at-risk groups					
	e.g., Develop a document or provide evidence on how you ensure these specific interview questions are used in recruitment.				
Section E: Risk Management (Priority standard)					
Standard 12: Have a comprehensive and effective risk management framework in place that includes reference to SEAH and a detailed risk register for the project					
	e.g., Develop a risk management policy or framework that captures SEAH risks.				
	e.g., Conduct an SEAH risk assessment of the proposed activities with details of the SEAH mitigation actions you will put in place.				
Standard 13: Have a detailed register of SEAH issues raised and how they were dealt with should be confidentially kept					
	e.g., Develop an SEAH cases register for your project that includes actions taken.				
	e.g., Demonstrate how this is kept confidential.				
Section F: Working with subcontractors and suppliers					
Standard 14: Include information on SEAH risks and expectations in contracts					
	e.g., Review or develop contracts that include information on SEAH risks and expectations.				
	e.g., Develop a plan for how you will monitor SEAH risks and mitigation actions in the project.				
Standard 15: Review subcontractors' policies against these minimum standards or similar					
	e.g., Develop or review the process you use to audit subcontractors' and suppliers' SEAH measures.				

continued on next page

continued from previous page

Identified SEAH Gap	Identified Action or Strategies	Target Output/s	Timeline and Date to be Completed	Person and Unit Responsible	Budget or Estimated Cost
	e.g., Develop or review the process to be followed where a subcontractor or supplier does not have appropriate SEAH policies and practices in place.				
Standard 16: Inform contractors and suppliers about project reporting mechanisms and the need to ensure these are in place					
	e.g., Develop a communication plan to ensure subcontractors and suppliers understand the project reporting systems and have integrated them into the project.				
Section G: Workplace Design					
Standard 17: Include SEAH in regular workplace safety assessments, including working accommodation, transportation, and site safety					
	e.g., Review or develop workplace safety assessments to include SEAH.				
	e.g., Develop a plan for how you monitor and review workplace safety assessments.				
Section H: Leadership and Accountability (Priority standard)					
Standard 18: Communication from the leadership of the contractor regarding its zero tolerance toward SEAH should occur regularly and utilize internal and external communication routes					
	e.g., Develop a communication plan for leadership to communicate SEAH zero-tolerance to the workforce.				
Standard 19: Have clear guidelines for monitoring and overseeing implementation of the policy or policies					
	e.g., Review or develop the process for monitoring implementation of SEAH policies.				
Standard 20: Have the capacity to report allegations to the executing and implementing agencies within 24 hours					
	e.g., Review or develop processes and agreements between you and your subcontractors and suppliers to report SEAH concerns and for this information to be shared with executing and implementing agencies in a timely manner.				
	e.g., Designate a dedicated person or persons to be tasked with reporting any arising SEAH breaches to the executing and implementing agencies.				
	e.g., Develop terms of reference and designate a person or team responsible for coordinating responses and planning actions to investigate and address corrective action related to SEAH breaches.				

Example Code of Conduct Regarding Sexual Exploitation, Abuse, and Harassment[1]

Note to the Employer:
This annex contains an example code of conduct that contractors can use if they do not have one already in place. Some contractors may already have a code of conduct in place, but it may not include sexual exploitation, abuse, and harassment (SEAH) issues or may not be as comprehensive in its approach to SEAH as the example in this annex. Contractors should ensure that their codes of conduct are as stringent as the one in this example. The following minimum requirements must not be modified. The employer may add additional requirements to address specific issues, informed by an assessment of project-specific risks. The types of issues identified could include risks associated with labor influx, the spread of communicable diseases, and specific forms of SEAH known to take place in the project context. The code of conduct should be a condition of employment.

Note to the Executing Agency and Implementing Agency:
Contractors should ensure that their codes of conduct are of equivalent stringency as the one in this example. The executing agency and/or implementing agency may add requirements as appropriate, including those related to contract-specific issues and SEAH risks. The contractor must initial and submit the code of conduct form as part of its bid. During implementation, a written code of conduct, translated in the dominant local language, should be displayed in an area that is highly visible and accessible to most of the workers.

We the Contractor [*enter name of Contractor*] have signed a contract with [*enter name of Employer*] for [*enter description of the Works*]. These Works will be carried out at [*enter the Site and other locations where the Works will be carried out*].

Our contract requires us to implement measures to address sexual exploitation, abuse, and harassment (SEAH). This Code of Conduct is part of our measures to address risks related to SEAH within the contracted project. It applies to all our staff, laborers, and other workers 24 hours a day, 7 days a week, both inside and outside of working hours. It also applies to the personnel of each subcontractor and any other personnel assisting us in the execution of the project. All such persons are referred to as "Contractor's Personnel" and are subject to this Code of Conduct. This Code of Conduct identifies the behavior that we require from all Contractor's Personnel.

Our workplace is an environment where unsafe, offensive, abusive, or violent behavior will not be tolerated and where all persons should feel comfortable raising issues or concerns without fear of retaliation.

All staff are required to read and/or understand this Code of Conduct prior to their employment starting with [*enter name of Contractor*] on the project.

---

[1] The information in this annex is adapted from Girls' Education Challenge. 2021. *GEC Fund Manager and Associated Personnel Safeguarding Policy*. London; and World Bank. 2020. *Addressing Sexual Exploitation and Abuse and Sexual Harassment (SEA/SH) in Investment Project Financing Involving Major Civil Works*. Second Edition. Washington, DC.

Contractor's Personnel shall:

- Carry out their duties competently and diligently.
- Comply with this Code of Conduct and all applicable laws, regulations, and other requirements, including requirements to protect the health, safety, and well-being of other Contractor's Personnel and any other person.
- Treat all people with respect and not discriminate against specific groups such as women; people with disabilities; members of lesbian, gay, bisexual, transgender, and queer/questioning (one's sexual or gender identity) communities; migrant workers; or children.
- Report work situations that they believe may violate this Code of Conduct using reporting mechanisms provided by the Contract.
- Uphold the rights and welfare of colleagues and project communities.
- Read thoroughly, promote, and raise awareness of all SEAH-related policies.
- Ensure they have received the relevant training on joining.
- Ensure they are aware of reporting mechanisms available to them and report any issues or causes for concern where they know or suspect that another contractor personnel has breached this Code of Conduct.
- Maintain confidentiality regarding concerns and report concerns using the reporting mechanisms provided only (e.g., not disclose their concerns beyond that reporting mechanism). This protects the dignity and identity of the alleged survivor and the alleged wrongdoer.

Contractor's Personnel shall not:

- Engage in sexual exploitation, which means any actual or attempted abuse of position of vulnerability, differential power, or trust, for sexual purposes, including, but not limited to, profiting monetarily, socially, or politically from the sexual exploitation of another.
- Engage in rape, which means physically forced or otherwise coerced penetration. The attempt to do so is known as attempted rape. Rape may be perpetrated by two or more perpetrators.
- Engage in sexual assault, which means any form of nonconsensual sexual contact that does not result in or include penetration. Examples include attempted rape, as well as unwanted kissing, fondling, or touching.
- Engage in any sexual activity with children according to the legal framework of the country. Mistaken belief regarding the age of a child is not a defense.
- Engage in any sexual activity with anyone who is unable to provide informed consent.
- Exchange money, employment, goods, or services for sex, including sexual favors or other forms of humiliating, degrading, or exploitative behavior.
- Engage in any other form of sexual exploitation or abuse.
- Engage in sexual harassment of any form, including but not limited to actions such as sexually suggestive gestures; comments on a worker's appearance, age, or private life; sexual comments, stories, and jokes; unwanted sexual advances; or revealing or discussing a person's sexual orientation or gender identity without their express permission.
- Openly display pictures, posters, graffiti, written materials, e-mails, or digital media that might be offensive to some, including sexually explicit or suggestive materials.
- Place phone calls or send messages on voice mail, or e-mail, or computer networks that are demeaning, threatening, abusive, humiliating, or offensive to staff.
- Engage in any form of sexual relationship with a person that they line manage or supervise.

- Neglect or choose not to declare, in the soonest time, romantic and/or sexual relationships with other staff to respective line manager, even if the relationship is at an early stage and may not continue.
- Use offensive, derogatory language or intimidating actions or behaviors.
- Insult or use threatening gestures or language (overt or implied).
- Be physically or emotionally abusive in any way.
- Persistently follow or stalk within the workplace, to and from work, or in other places even outside working hours.
- Retaliate against any person who reports violations of this Code of Conduct.

If working with children present, Contractor's Personnel shall:

- Not work alone with children and plan their work so that at least two adults are present at any time.
- Behave appropriately, ensure that language is moderated in their presence, and refrain from adult jokes or comments that may cause discomfort or offense.
- Avoid inappropriate physical contact with a child. Using common sense, this does not limit physical contact with a child or adult at risk if they are hurt or distressed. In this circumstance, a child may be comforted or reassured without compromising their dignity.
- Be sensitive to local norms and standards of behavior toward children. Where local norms and standards of behavior contravene this Code of Conduct, the Contractor's policies and standards take precedence.
- Never act in a way that may be abusive or may place a child at risk of abuse.
- Not expose children to materials with sexual content.
- Not condone, nor participate in, behavior against a child that is illegal, unsafe, or abusive.
- Never hit or otherwise physically assault, harm, or abuse them.
- Not develop physical or sexual relationships with a child.
- Never verbally or physically act in a manner that is inappropriate or sexually provocative.
- Not develop relationships with them that could in any way be deemed exploitative or abusive.
- Not use language, make suggestions, or offer advice that is inappropriate, offensive, or abusive.
- Never act in ways intended to shame, humiliate, belittle, or degrade children or otherwise perpetrate any form of emotional abuse, discriminate against, show differential treatment, or favor particular children to the exclusion of others.
- Never allow allegations made by a child, or concerns expressed by others about their welfare, to go unrecorded or not acted upon.
- Not have a child stay overnight at your home or other personal accommodation in which you are staying.
- Never use a computer or other electronic device to view, download, distribute, or create indecent or inappropriate images of children- or adults-at-risk.
- Never engage in any commercially exploitative activities with children including child labor or trafficking.

In addition, Line Managers must always:

- Create a safe environment where staff and others feel able to raise concerns without fear of retribution.
- Ensure that if a member of their team has reported a breach of this Code of Conduct, it is raised with the formal reporting mechanism within 24 hours.
- Ensure all staff members and contractors that they manage are trained on the Code of Conduct and procedures within 2 weeks of starting employment.
- Ensure that staff are aware of referral services for health, legal, and psychosocial support to provide to anyone disclosing.
- Set a positive example both on and off duty.

Consequences of violating the Code of Conduct:

Any violation of this Code of Conduct by Contractor's Personnel may result in serious consequences, up to and including termination and possible referral to legal authorities.

Raising Concerns:

If any person observes behavior that they believe may represent a violation of this Code of Conduct, or that otherwise concerns them, they should raise the issue promptly. This can be done in either of the following ways:

[Insert here the reporting mechanisms in place]

Declaration:

I have received a copy of this Code of Conduct written in a language that I comprehend.
I understand that if I have any questions about this Code of Conduct, I can contact *[enter name of Contractor's contact person with relevant experience in handling SEAH]* requesting an explanation.

Name of Contractor's Personnel: *[insert name]* _____

Signature: _____

Date: (day / month / year): _____

Countersignature of authorized representative of the Contractor: _____

Signature: _____

Date: (day / month / year): _____

Service Mapping Guidance

It is prudent to have a strong sexual exploitation, abuse, and harassment (SEAH) response service referral pathway for each project. This should be compiled for every location in which the project works. Health, mental health, psychosocial, and legal services should be in place. This guidance provides templates for executing agencies, implementing agencies, and contractors to use when mapping services and assessing the strength and accessibility of that service. Executing and implementing agencies can use this guidance and template to assess the existence and strength of services within accessible reach of a project site (within 4 hours' travel time).

Contractors or third-party SEAH service providers should use this mapping to develop their trusted referral pathway for projects, where the highest quality services are those the contractors most commonly refer survivors to. Contractors may choose to partner with suitable services as the third-party responder for their project. They should also consider putting in place information sharing protocols so that SEAH survivors who disclose directly to them may choose to have the service provider report to the contractor on their behalf.[1]

Executing and implementing agencies can also use this mapping to develop an understanding of what is needed to fill gaps in service provision and incorporate this information into their plans and budget.

During project preparation, basic service mapping is required for all projects and a more thorough service mapping is required for projects rated substantial- and high-risk.[2] Being able to refer SEAH survivors to safe and appropriate services is of the utmost importance.

Mapping should include an assessment of access to quality services. It is likely that this information can be sourced from relevant national and local government departments and nongovernment organizations.

SEAH survivors often need various types of care and support to help them recover and heal and to be safe from further violence. Some of the most common services that survivors have the right to receive are as follows:

- **Medical and health.** Medical treatment and health care address the immediate and long-term physical and mental health effects of gender-based violence (GBV). This can include initial examination and treatment; follow-up medical care; mental health care; and health-related legal services, such as the preparation of documentation and provision of evidence during judicial and related processes.

---

[1] For further information on information sharing protocols see http://www.gbvims.com/wp/wp-content/uploads/7-Inter-Agency-ISP-Template_v6.doc.

[2] For more details, see pp. 25–26 of this good practice note.

- **Psychosocial.** Psychosocial care and support assist with healing and recovery from emotional, psychological, and social effects. This includes crisis care and longer-term emotional and practical support for the survivor and their family, information and advocacy, specialist social worker management of the survivor's recovery, and education of family members so that they can support the survivor's healing and recovery. These psychosocial support services are often provided through specialist social worker management of the survivor's recovery process, or through other individual and group services provided by the same organization.

- **Safety and protection.** Options may be needed for the safety and protection for survivors and their families who are at risk of further violence and who wish to be protected. These can include safe shelters; police or community security; relocation; and, in the case of children, alternative care arrangements.

- **Legal services.** Legal and law enforcement services can promote or help survivors to claim their legal rights and protections. They include criminal investigation, protection and prosecution, legal aid services, and court support.

- **Education and livelihood.** Education and livelihood opportunities support survivors and their families to live independently and in safety and dignity. They can include referral pathways for existing livelihood and education programs or services, nonformal education and adult learning options, and targeted economic interventions that can mitigate risks of GBV and foster healing and empowerment.

- **Other services.** Other protection services include durable solutions for displaced populations. In displacement situations, lack of documentation and detention can expose survivors to considerable further risk. Planning for durable solutions, including resettlement, local integration, and voluntary repatriation can contribute significantly to a survivor's safety.

- **Specialist services.** These include services for at-risk groups; women's groups; groups working with people with diverse sexual orientation, gender identity and expression, and sexual characteristics; disability rights groups; and minority groups who may face language barriers.

- **Child protection specialist services.** These specialist services provide protection for children who are at risk of or are experiencing neglect, physical, sexual, or emotional abuse. This may include screening and investigation of reports of child abuse, assessment of safety and risks, and provision of referrals to services and resources to children and their families.

Sexual Exploitation, Abuse, and Harassment Services Mapping and Gap Analysis Tool

1. Health

Item	Answer Options	Answer	Detailed Notes
Details of service	Name of service institution		
	Address		
	Contact		
	Name of contact person within service		
	Opening hours		
Physical accessibility			
Average distance from the project site (kilometers [km] or time)	Maximum distance to be traveled (km)		
Do people with disabilities have access?	Car journey time		
	Ramp access? (Y/N)		
	Disability inclusive washrooms? (Y/N)		
Services			
Health care can be accessed without police involvement.	Yes/No/Partially		
Health care can be accessed without payment or specific documentation that survivors may not have.	Yes/No/Partially		
A safe and private environment is available for medical examination and treatment.	Yes/No/Partially		
Health workers are trained in confidentiality.	Yes/No/Partially		
Doctors or nurses have been trained in the clinical care of sexual assault, including for children.	Yes/No/Partially		
Protocols for clinical management of rape survivors are in place and followed.	Yes/No/Partially		
Medical examination and treatment are provided by trained staff.	Yes/No/Partially		
Appropriate equipment and supplies, including medications or drugs, are available.[a]	Yes/No/Partially		
Patients are referred for additional health care as needed.	Yes/No/Partially		
Follow-up health care is provided.	Yes/No/Partially		
Health workers know how to give information and are guided by protocols on referrals for protection, safety, and psychosocial support.	Yes/No/Partially		

continued on next page

continued from previous page

Item	Answer Options	Answer	Detailed Notes
Interpretation is available for survivors who do not speak the same language as the health care workers (where necessary).	Yes/No/Partially		
Mental health services are available for survivors.[b]	Yes/No/Partially		
Health care services are accessible to all survivors, regardless of gender, sexual orientation, gender identity and expression, ethnic or religious background, etc.	Yes/No/Partially		
The project-affected community is aware of the services.	Yes/No/Partially		
Medical certificate and other medical records are available to the survivor at no extra cost.	Yes/No/Partially		

2. Mental Health and Psychosocial

Question	Answer Options	Answer	Detailed Notes
Details of service	Name of service institution		
	Address		
	Contact		
	Name of contact person within service		
	Opening hours		
Physical Accessibility			
Average distance from the project site (km and time)	Maximum distance to be traveled (km)		
	Car journey time		
Do people with disabilities have access to special care?	Ramp access? (Y/N)		
	Disability inclusive washrooms? (Y/N)		
Services			
A safe and private environment allows people to receive compassionate assistance.	Yes/No/Partially		
Staff and/or volunteers are trained in confidentiality.	Yes/No/Partially		
Trained staff and/or volunteers can provide relevant information and are guided by protocols on referrals for health care, police, and safety options to people seeking help.	Yes/No/Partially		

continued on next page

continued from previous page

Question	Answer Options	Answer	Detailed Notes
There are staff and/or volunteers who are representative of the different ethnic and religious backgrounds relevant to the context.	Yes/No/Partially		
Trained staff/volunteers are able to provide basic crisis support to individuals and families.	Yes/No/Partially		
Trained staff and/or volunteers can provide case management to survivors.	Yes/No/Partially		
Resources are available to meet immediate basic needs, e.g., clothing and food.	Yes/No/Partially		
Short-term safety options are available in the community.	Yes/No/Partially		
Trained staff and/or volunteers are available to provide information and education to families of survivors.	Yes/No/Partially		
Group activities are available for peer support, community reintegration, and promoting economic empowerment.	Yes/No/Partially		
Traditional healing or cleansing practices that survivors perceive as helpful in their recovery and that promote the human rights of survivors are considered appropriate.	Yes/No/Partially		
Interpretation is available for survivors who do not speak the same language as workers (where necessary).	Yes/No/Partially		
Community outreach and education about GBV takes place	Yes/No/Partially		
Health care services are accessible to all survivors, regardless of gender, sexual orientation, gender identity and expression, ethnic or religious background, etc.	Yes/No/Partially		
The project-affected community is aware of the services.	Yes/No/Partially		

3. Law Enforcement

Question	Answer Options	Answer	Detailed Notes
Details of service	Name of service institution		
	Address		
	Contact		
	Name of contact person within service		
	Opening hours		

continued on next page

continued from previous page

Question	Answer Options	Answer	Detailed Notes
Physical Accessibility			
Average distance from the project site (km and time)	Maximum distance to be traveled (km)		
	Car journey time		
People with disabilities have access.	Ramp access? (Y/N)		
	Disability inclusive washrooms? (Y/N)		
Services			
A women's and children's or GBV desk is present and operational.	Yes/No/Partially		
Procedures for reporting complaints to police promote dignity and confidentiality.	Yes/No/Partially		
Survivors are not likely to be subject to arrest or detention based on legal status or any other characteristic upon reporting to police.	Yes/No/Partially		
Interviews and investigations are conducted by police officers trained to handle SEAH-related complaints, preferably of the same sex as the survivor.	Yes/No/Partially		
Investigative techniques promote dignity of survivors, for example in how survivors are spoken to and treated.	Yes/No/Partially		
Police have the capacity to respond promptly to criminal allegations of GBV.	Yes/No/Partially		
Testimonial evidence is recorded properly, and the integrity of physical and documentary evidence gathered are securely preserved.	Yes/No/Partially		
Police procedures, including decisions on arrest, detention, and the terms under which perpetrators may be released, consider the safety of the survivor and others.	Yes/No/Partially		
Training and education on GBV are provided to police, criminal justice officials, and practitioners and professionals involved in the criminal justice system.	Yes/No/Partially		
Certified copies of evidence gathered by the police are available to the victim–survivor at no cost.	Yes/No/Partially		

4. Legal Services and Justice

Question	Answer Options	Answer	Detailed Notes
Details of service	Name		
	Address		
	Contact		
	Name of contact person within service		
	Opening hours		
Physical Accessibility			
Average distance from the project site (km and time)	Maximum distance to be traveled (km)		
	Car journey time		
People with disabilities have access.	Ramp access? (Y/N)		
	Disability inclusive washrooms? (Y/N)		
Services			
Legal counseling is available to advise survivors of their legal rights and remedies and on the process for criminal, civil, administrative, or other proceedings.	Yes/No/Partially		
Legal representation is available and accessible.	Yes/No/Partially		
Practical (e.g., transportation) and emotional support is available for victims and witnesses to attend court.	Yes/No/Partially		
Court mechanisms and procedures are accessible and observe rules on confidentiality, privacy, and protection against re-traumatization of survivors.	Yes/No/Partially		

[a] For details on drug protocols see World Health Organization (WHO), United Nations Population Fund, and United Nations High Commissioner for Refugees. 2019. Clinical Management of Rape and Intimate Partner Violence Survivors: Developing Protocols for Use in Humanitarian Settings. Geneva: WHO.

[b] This is to assess whether mental health services exist within a health setting. A form to assess the suitability of mental health services is in part 2 of the table: Mental Health and Psychosocial.

Source: Adapted from Gender-Based Violence Information Management System Steering Committee. 2017. Interagency Gender-Based Violence Case Management Guidelines: Providing Care and Case Management Services to Gender-Based Violence Survivors in Humanitarian Settings. First Edition.

Name of Project: _____

Location: _____

Name of Contractor: _____

Contact Details: _____

Approved for Submission by [Name]: _____

Designation: _____

Date Submitted: _____

Name of Executing Agency and Implementing Agency: _____

Reviewed and Approved by [Name]: _____

Designation: _____

Date Approved: _____

Key Guiding Questions When Reviewing a Project In-Depth Sexual Exploitation, Abuse, and Harassment Analysis and Assessment Report

When preparing a project, particularly during the due diligence process, executing and/or implementing agencies will be required to undertake a sexual exploitation, abuse, and harassment (SEAH) analysis or in-depth assessment of projects categorized as *substantial* or *high*-risk. This assessment will be conducted by consultant SEAH specialists. It would be useful for ADB staff members and SEAH focal points in the executing and implementing agencies to assure the quality of the analysis, particularly where they have been conducted by social and/or gender specialists working on *low* and *moderate* risk projects. The questions in this annex have been designed to help understand what to look for in an externally commissioned SEAH analysis, and to be a useful reference for the development of terms of reference.

National analysis. Guiding questions to consider when reviewing a national SEAH analysis include the following:

- Does the analysis include information on the scale and nature of SEAH?
- Does it set out the legal framework at the national level with regards to SEAH, including the relevant rights of women and girls and boys and the nature of any gaps?
- Does it explain the drivers and risk factors that sustain SEAH?
- Does it set out which groups of women and girls are most vulnerable to experiencing SEAH and why they are most at risk? Does it set out which groups of men and boys are most vulnerable to experiencing SEAH and why they are most at risk?
- Does the analysis outline what happens to women and girls who have reported SEAH, including where they go for help?
- Does the analysis discuss the potential risks and consequences for women and girls of reporting SEAH?

Site analysis. Guiding questions to consider when reviewing SEAH analysis at project implementation sites include the following:

- Does the analysis clearly present which actors (e.g., local government, service providers, women's rights organizations, child protection organizations, and nongovernment organizations) are working on SEAH or other forms of violence in the location(s) where the project will be implemented?
- Does the analysis set out how SEAH is manifesting in the targeted communities?
- Does the analysis explain the social norms in the project sites in relation to SEAH?
- Does the analysis outline what services or programs are in place for survivors of SEAH and what the major gaps in service provision are including in relation to medical, legal, psychosocial, shelter, and child-specific services? Is it clear whether these services are accessible to different groups of survivors such as people with disabilities, HIV positive individuals, women and girls, and children?
- Has the current capacity of key stakeholders working on SEAH near the project location been analyzed?
- Has the analysis examined current or planned initiatives to strengthen SEAH service provision in the targeted communities?

Project analysis. Guiding questions to consider when reviewing the recommended actions for SEAH prevention, mitigation, and response for a project include the following:

- Has the analysis proposed prevention, mitigation, and response actions for all SEAH risks identified?
- Are the recommended actions in line with work already going on in the community in relation to aligning the grievance redress mechanism? Have the recommended actions leveraged on scaling communities for ADB to work jointly with other actors in the communities?
- Are the recommended actions likely to lead to prevention and mitigation of SEAH?
- Are the recommended actions likely to result in survivors of SEAH being able to access a comprehensive package of support in a survivor-centered way? Do the recommended actions include reference to how child survivors of SEAH will be supported?
- Are the recommended actions built around information collected from those most likely to be affected by SEAH, such as women, people affected by displacement, the poorest individuals, and those with disabilities?

Examples of Data Collection Methods for Analysis or In-Depth Assessments of Sexual Exploitation, Abuse, and Harassment Risks

For projects categorized *substantial* or *high*-risk it is prudent to prepare an in-depth sexual exploitation, abuse, and harassment (SEAH) risk assessment report as part of due diligence. Data gathered from this assessment will inform the project SEAH plan on how and where services may be provided if SEAH occurs.

Data Collection Methods for Sexual Exploitation, Abuse, and Harassment Analysis and In-Depth Assessments

Method	Materials to review and examples of Stakeholders to include
Desk review	• Review existing ADB assessment materials relating to sexual exploitation, abuse, and harassment (SEAH); gender-based violence; and gender. • Use materials listed in the "country context" tab of the risk calculator.
Key informant interviews	• Worker representatives and trade unions • Staff from local women's rights organizations and organizations representing other groups such as organizations of people with disabilities and lesbian, gay, bisexual, transgender, and queer/questioning (LGBTQI) rights organizations. • Staff from international and local nongovernment organizations working on gender-based violence and/or SEAH • Health workers on site or in local communities • Representatives of government agencies
Focus group discussions	• Community leaders and members (various genders and ages). • Service users and user groups • Women-only focus group discussions
Observations	Location and design of worksites and services (e.g., isolated and poorly lit spaces) Proximity of worksites to communities, schools, and health centers

Source: S. Neville et al. 2020. *Addressing Gender-Based Violence and Harassment: Emerging Good Practice for the Private Sector*. European Bank for Reconstruction and Development, CDC, and International Finance Corporation.

Monitoring Guidance

Monitoring visits offer opportunities for staff or consultants of the executing and implementing agencies to observe project practices and ask clarifying questions to understand how a project is approaching sexual exploitation, abuse, and harassment (SEAH) prevention, mitigation, and response. Even if it is not possible to ask the contractor's project team specific SEAH questions, observations can offer useful information about a project's work on SEAH.

During the monitoring visits,

(i) be alert to situations that may constitute SEAH or other forms of workplace misconduct, breaches to the code of conduct, or harm to community members because of the project; if staff have any concerns about the immediate safety of any individual or groups based on observations during a monitoring visit, this must be escalated immediately via the appropriate SEAH reporting mechanism;

(ii) look for any information (such as posters) about how to report a concern, including in relation to SEAH, and check whether it is this accessible to the contractor's staff and community members; and

(iii) look for any incidents of (not employed) women and children hanging around the project site.

If time and the context of a visit allows, it can be useful to ask contractors' staff specific questions on SEAH. The checklist in the table offers examples of questions that can be used and what might constitute adequate response.

Possible Questions for Sexual Exploitation, Abuse, and Harassment Monitoring Visits

Example Question	What to Look For (Observations and Answers)
Do all project financed contractors' staff know what is in the code of conduct?	Staff at all levels and across all contractors should be able to speak to some minimum standards on SEAH, such as that sexual harassment is not permitted and how they would raise a concern. As a result, staff should try to speak to different types of workers (from senior to junior) to check their knowledge of and confidence in the project's approach to SEAH prevention, mitigation, and response. They should be able to at least articulate what acts constitute SEAH.
Do all staff, contractors, and community members know how to report a concern (for example of sexual harassment)?	For grievance redress mechanisms (GRMs) to be effective, they must be widely accessible to staff, contractors, and community members. Staff should try to speak to different groups of individuals to see if they know how to report and incident. If some groups do not, it is an indication that the GRM is not functioning. The GRM must also contain multiple ways of reporting. Staff should observe any efforts to raise awareness of the GRM (such as a poster on the project site).
Have all relevant staff of contractors had training on SEAH?	Staff of the executing agency, implementing agency, and consultants should try to verify what training the contractor's personnel have received in relation to SEAH and when they received it. Have records been kept for staff completing the training? Have new staff been receiving the training during their induction?

continued on next page

continued from previous page

Example Question	What to Look For (Observations and Answers)
How does the response mechanism work?	Executing and implementing agency staff and consultants should attempt to check how cases are logged. For example, is confidentiality kept at all times? Has the service mapping been updated and is it easily accessible? Has the person responding to complaints been trained on handling SEAH cases and interacting with survivors? Executing and implementing agency staff members can ask the health and safety officer (or other relevant person) to walk them through each step of what a response to an SEAH concern should look like.
How is the contractor working to prevent and mitigate SEAH?	Refer to the contractor SEAH action plan and confirm that the contractor's team is aware of the identified SEAH risks and what activities have been planned to prevent, mitigate, and respond to concerns. Are these progressing according to the work plan?

Source: Asian Development Bank.

Template for Assessment of Potential Risks Associated with Case Handling

Reporting and responding to sexual exploitation, abuse, and harassment incidents may involve multiple risks to the individuals involved. To ensure the response process considers individual protection needs, a designated focal point who is appointed to receive complaints and log them in a central register should complete a risk assessment. This should be performed at the initial reporting stage and updated regularly throughout the case handling process. The table shows some examples of potential risks. However, the risk assessment for each incident must consider whether there are other risks specific to the case.

Template for Assessing Risks Associated with Case Handling

No.	Risk	Likelihood (1–5, with 5 being most likely)	Predicted Impact/ Effect	Recommended Mitigation Measure	Responsibility
1	Survivors are negatively impacted by the investigation process, e.g., by being stigmatized, bullied, losing their job, and other acts of retaliation against the survivor by the subject of concern, staff, or community.				
2	The identity of complainant or whistleblower becomes known.				
3	Staff and/or community retaliate against the subject of concern.				
4	Breaches of conduct are found to extend beyond the current allegations.				
5	The subject of concern abuses or harasses vulnerable populations.				
6	There is reputational risk to the contractor, executing agency, implementing agency, or Asian Development Bank.				
7	There is an information breach.				
8	The subject of concern contacts witnesses and/or others involved in the investigation.				
9	The survivor does not wish to engage with the investigation.				
10	Other risks to the survivor or the subject of concern.				

Source: Asian Development Bank.

Name of Project: _____

Location: _____

Name of contractor: _____

Contact details: _____

Prepared by [Name]: _____

Designation: _____

Date prepared: _____

Sexual Exploitation, Abuse, and Harassment Incident Reporting Form Template

This four-part form is recommended for reporting sexual exploitation, abuse, and harassment concerns.

Incident Reporting Form

Part 1: Initial Report Form

No.	Item	Response
1.	This sexual exploitation, abuse, and harassment (SEAH) incident relates to (Project Name)	
2.	Reference number used by the executing and/or implementing agencies	
3.	Date SEAH incident or issue was first reported	
4.	SEAH incident details (summary)	
5.	Are there additional risks to the health, safety, or wellbeing of the alleged survivor or survivors?	
6.	If "yes," what are these risks, and in what way have you mitigated them? If "no" or "unknown," please elaborate if you can.	
7.	Does the incident or issue present a risk to the health, safety, or wellbeing of other people?	
8.	If "yes," what are these risks, and in what way have you mitigated them? If "no" or "unknown," please elaborate if you can.	
9.	If "yes," who is at risk?	
10.	Is there a risk to the project or reputational risks for the Asian Development Bank (ADB)?	
11.	If "yes," what is the risk?	
12.	Name and position of person reporting	
13.	Date submitted	

Part 2: Further Details (to be submitted within 24 hours of initial report form)

No.	Item	Response
1.	Organization(s) involved and their relationship to ADB funding	
2.	Number of alleged survivors	
3.	Age of alleged survivor(s) (approximate age is acceptable)	
4.	Gender of alleged survivor(s)	
5.	Is the alleged survivor a person with a disability?	
6.	Do the alleged survivor(s) identify as lesbian, gay, bisexual, transgender, and queer/questioning (LGBTQI)?	
7.	Do the alleged survivor(s) identify as an ethnic minority or indigenous person? If yes specify	
8.	Are the alleged survivor(s) being resettled as a part of the ADB project?	
9.	What is the role of the subject of concern within the project?	
10.	Any further details regarding subject of concern	
11.	Country	
12.	Region, state, or province	
13.	Location of incident	
14.	Date incident took place (if known)	
15.	Who reported the concern?	
16.	How was the concern or incident reported?	
17.	Confirm whether the incident is a crime according to local law	
18.	Confirm whether incident was reported to the authorities	
19.	If "yes," confirm date of report and where and to whom the report was made	
20.	If "no," confirm why this was not reported (e.g., it was not illegal, the survivor did not wish to report to the authorities, or it was not safe for the survivor to report)	
21.	Detailed description of incident	
22.	Immediate actions taken with regards to the alleged survivor(s)	
23.	Are the alleged survivor(s) now safe? (e.g., from retributive action from perpetrator, their friends, and/or family; and from further traumatization resulting from incident)	
24.	Details of survivor assistance provided	
25.	Immediate actions taken with regards to the subject of concern	
26.	Name and position of person completing part 2 of this form	
27.	Date submitted	

Part 3: Investigation Planning (to be completed within 1 week of report being made)

No.	Item	Response
1.	Investigation terms of reference (attachment)	
2.	Investigation team details, positions, and qualifications	
3.	Timeframe for concluding the investigation	
4.	Name and position of person completing part 3 of this form	
5.	Date submitted	

Part 4: Investigation and Closure Report

No.	Question	Response
1.	Describe the investigation process used, why this methodology was chosen, and whether this was successful	
2.	Outcome of investigation	
3.	Individuals involved in the outcome	
4.	Follow-up actions by the project and relevant organization	
5.	Status of the alleged survivor(s)	
6.	Has the project identified health, psychosocial, legal, protection, livelihoods, and other relevant services to refer survivor(s) to; and has the referral been made for longer-term support if needed?	
7.	Outcome regarding subject of concern	
8.	Lessons learned and project adaptations	
9.	Name and position of person completing part 4 of this form	
10.	Date submitted	

Name of Project: _____

Location: _____

Name of executing agency and implementing agency: _____

Contact details: _____

Approved for submission by [*Name*]**:** _____

Designation: _____

Date submitted: _____